ENLIGHTENED MASTER SEEKS APPRENTICE

Learn to Transform Your Burning
Desire into The Greatness You Seek.

STEVE BODE

ISBN: 978-1-7342156-1-8

Cover Design by @FastDesign360
Interior Design by www.FormattedBooks.com Editing by *Janna Rasch*
Written by Steve Bode www.TheNudge.Club

To contact the author, please email at stevebode8@hotmail.com

DEDICATION

A few years ago, I was looking for something. It was nothing more than a vague idea, but I knew it was big—not just for me, but for everyone. I wanted change, improvement, and to reach something closer to my true potential. Back then, I wasn't sure where it was, how to get there, or if what I was searching for was even possible. Now, I'm certain that it is. I gained this certainty by listening to what others before me had to say about the same thing I had—the need to improve.

I rolled up my sleeves and started listening to and reading as many books as possible. My unachievable goal is to go through every book on improvement ever written.

The human mind processes about 70,000 thoughts per day. By the age of 40, that's over a trillion thoughts. There are as many neurons firing in your brain as there are stars in the Universe. The capacity is unimaginable. I'm pretty sure that my brain can assimilate every book ever written about the subject of self-improvement, so I set out to do it. I have yet to finish, but something has happened to me along the way. I stopped the endless thought loops I was stuck in, and I started creating new, innovative thoughts and implementing them in my life. I believe I changed on an atomic level, and it's because so many authors wanted to share what they have learned.

This book is dedicated to those that have given of themselves to make the lives of others better. It's easiest for me to thank the authors of the books that I have read, but this goes much deeper. It's for anyone and everyone that has made an improvement in someone's life—the bigger, the better.

Here are some of my favorite authors and their websites:

Antonio Damasio - https://www.antoniodamasio.com
Charles Duhigg - https://charlesduhigg.com
Christina R. Wodtke - http://cwodtke.com
Daniel Goleman Ph.D. - http://www.danielgoleman.info
David Eagleman - https://www.eagleman.com
Dean Graziosi - https://www.deangraziosi.com
Dr. Rebecca Newton - https://rebeccanewton.co.uk
Dr. Caroline Leaf - https://drleaf.com
Dr. Joe Dispenza - https://drjoedispenza.com
Eric Barker - https://www.bakadesuyo.com
Gary Vaynerchuk - https://www.garyvaynerchuk.com
Grant Cardone - https://grantcardone.com
Greg McKeown - https://gregmckeown.com
Hal Elrod - https://halelrod.com
Ian Tuhovsky - http://www.mindfulnessforsuccess.com
James Clear - https://jamesclear.com
Jeff Haden - https://www.jeffhaden.com
Jen Sincero - https://jensincero.com
John C. Maxwell - https://www.johnmaxwell.com
Kelly McGonigal Ph.D. - http://kellymcgonigal.com
Kindra Hall - https://kindrahall.com
Laura Vande.rkam - https://lauravanderkam.com
Lisa Wimberger - https://www.neurosculptinginstitute.com
Malcolm Gladwell - https://www.gladwellbooks.com
Nir Eyal - https://www.nirandfar.com
Peter Hollins - https://petehollins.com
Robert Greene - https://powerseductionandwar.com
Ryan Holiday - https://ryanholiday.net/about/
Steven Kotler - https://www.stevenkotler.com
Yuval Noah Harari - https://www.ynharari.com

Dear Reader,

Every great once in a while, someone emerges. Not just *someone*, but *the* one. They come from different places, different times, and for various reasons, appearing when things look their bleakest. They have some innate, burning desire to solve one thing—the most significant thing at the time. Sometimes it's tyranny, sometimes ignorance; other times it's a lack of peace. They not only change the way we think but also our very nature. They become folklore and legend. In reality, they're often simple, noble, and unassuming. History remembers them differently than they are, but there is a fundamental truth that never changes. The day-to-day story is often not so interesting, but these individuals' souls defy words.

A long time from now, civilization will never remember the struggles, the doubt, the lessons yet to be learned. They will only know the difference made.

They will remember your name—for it is you *and* me.

You have the potential to be that person that history will look back on with admiration.

What if right now you could reach back into your past? What would you tell yourself? What do you know now that you wished you knew then? How much different would things be? Would you have worked a little harder in school, learned to relax more around strangers, or been more guarded? Experience tells us how to prepare for the future. It's a survival mechanism—and it's worked. Everything that you are today is somehow based on your past, both genetically as a homo-sapiens, and how you run your daily life. Maybe you're a little more independent today because you had to be as a child just to survive, maybe you were given everything and now subconsciously expect the same as an adult. The past affects you, whether you are conscious of it or not.

As fun as it might be to explore what you'd tell your younger self, it doesn't change your past, but you can change your future by altering the path you're on. Where is your life headed? Is it the life you want?

What if your future self could tell you what you are doing wrong today or about to do wrong? What if in the future you achieve some level of enlightenment and you find a way to reach back into time and give yourself a nudge here and there. What if the ideas of this book is the voice of your future reaching back to you? Maybe it is, maybe it's not, but what if you thought of it that way. Will it sink in a little deeper?

Regardless there is something incredible about you, yet you only have a vague idea of what you are capable of. I know you have an innate feeling that you can achieve greatness, but you're spinning your wheels. You have tried and tried to escape the thought loops and feelings of helplessness to no avail. Maybe you have quit trying because getting by has become the main concern, but in moments of quiet, that little voice in your head wonders what happened to your childhood dreams?

It's not too late.

This book is an outline of things you can do to achieve your goals and reach a higher level of spiritual enlightenment.

First, you need to reach a stable point in life. Then, I'll show you what went wrong with you and with humanity. I'll give you an overview of how to use your brain and mind. Finally, I'll show you practical steps you can take that will help you achieve the greatness you seek if practiced regularly.

This book is your wake-up call, your destiny, and it's about time.

It's about *your time*, the time you waste as you fritter away the dreams you once had. You'll discover these truths on your own, but it'll be slow and full of heartache and frustration. I can see you're in some of that now. You feel a little lost, and just when you get things on the right track, something new pops up, and you're back to square one. Nothing will get better unless you make some real, unexpected changes.

You may have already mastered some of the techniques I'll give you. Others will take more effort. My quest is to challenge you to master this.

YOU HAVE GREATNESS
IN YOU

Enlightenment, in its simplest terms, is that feeling you have when you come to a truth. Sometimes it's subtle. Sometimes it's strong enough to knock you to your knees. The term originated in Europe in the 17th century. It was a further evolution of what we learned about ourselves during the Renaissance—the concept of letting go of ideas and opinions that you hold onto simply because you were told by an authority, like your parents, society, the church, or the king. Enlightenment was the idea of looking for and finding the real answers about life and why we are the way we are.

This was the time of the philosopher Voltaire and the mathematician Galileo Galilei. Voltaire was in no small part responsible for inciting the French to turn against the aristocracy. Galilei had a strong bond with the church and was friends with the Pope. Everything Galilei published was in direct contradiction with the church, and he was accused of heresy. Galileo's calculations flew directly in the face of what the church was telling us at the time—that the Earth was the center of God's creation.

Math, science, and reason were on their way in. Superstition and guessing were on their way out. The Rights of Man, a document that most democratic governments today are based on, was written. The idea of the authoritative class was being rebelled against.

Having that more profound understanding of what makes you tick is enlightenment. Becoming an Enlightened Master is having that deep understanding of who you are, and who we all are, and why the Universe is the way it is. It's not guessing or hypothesizing about these things, it's having the *knowledge* that you can readily get at the answers you seek, and you can differentiate the *not quite* feeling from *Sweet Holy Mother of God; I now know the meaning of Life.*

The benefits of enlightenment are beyond description with words, but this should give you some idea. You are no longer troubled by the chaos and unpredictability of life. You are always at peace, and solutions to the most challenging problems come to you quickly. You think more clearly and effectively. Your memory is superb, and you can pull data from the most obscure places in your mind to solve seemingly unsolvable problems. You are also less likely to get embroiled in emotions and won't use your emotions to try to solve problems.

I know you have great potential, but you've gotten lost. The world you live in is not set up to help you. I'm here to show you a path to that enlightened state. We all have that ability innately, but we subvert it simply because we don't know it's there. I am your guide.

It is no wonder we have gotten lost as individuals and as a society. We can look back into history and shake our heads in disbelief—yet it is genuinely real. As a society, we learn slowly, but things are changing at an exponential pace. Regardless of how evolved our society is, the way we teach ourselves and the way political parties treat us as a group is not far off from animal societies. There's a deeper source that drives our actions. When you see someone walking toward you on the sidewalk, you unconsciously and instantly size them up. Is he a threat? Is he suspicious, happy, someone you'd like to know? We do this on a gut level, well before any conscious thinking happens. It is the result of thousands of millions of years of evolution. It's there, but it is occluded from that thing that you think is *you*. It's subconscious.

Not only are the true source of our actions hidden, the further along we go, and the more momentum we build, it's becomes harder and harder to change. Humans have been evolving for 66 million years, and 3.5 billion years for life in general. We have a very long history. Change is easy when you're young or new, but the more mass accumulated and the more time it has been around, the less likely change occurs.

We see this evolution in business as well. When a company grows from 10 to 20,000 employees, making a change isn't so easy.

Our systems have evolved to keep us afloat, stable, and alive. You've been groomed to be a cog in the works, but you know deep down that you're destined for more. Significant leaps forward aren't possible while in the system, and the longer you're in, the more effort it takes to get out.

This is where you stand alone from your peers. I know you've always had a feeling that there's something bigger out there and that you can and should be a part of it. You know that there's more for you than what society has groomed you for: going to school, getting a job, buying a home, getting married, having kids, retiring, sitting around until you become too old to enjoy your time, then you move on. This is survival, and we are slowly getting better at it—but as with any evolution, it's one step at a time.

You have been taught that larger leaps aren't possible because you need to build one system on top of the next. You can't jump out of the system to be something more significant because you are part of the system. You are helping to hold it together. Your finger is plugging the hole in the leaking dam. I'm not asking you to pull your finger out of the dam, and I'm not asking you to leave your finger there while doing other things. I'm telling you that you are well above the damn dam. You've been given a problem and told that the only solution is to stay where you are. Both of those datums are false.

Now is the time. I have seen your future. I know your past struggles, and I know what you're in for. Part of me wishes it didn't take so long, but like in any evolution, lessons needed to be learned. It'll be challenging, but I know you make it to the other side.

Now, you are going to take a quantum leap forward. You'll skip some of the heartaches, worry, and struggles that your peers are facing. I'm grabbing you by the hand and pulling you forward. It is your time. Ready or not, let's go.

SETTING THE STAGE

Your life is as you decide. If that does not seem so, it is you who decided it so.

You are what you decide. More precisely, you are *because* you decide. With that, our inclination to be accepted by others has led us to become very much like each other. We want to look and act like those we admire, so we become more like them. We learn to be part of society and we find that it works. We are alive after all, and we decide that is enough. We move with society's flow and at its pace. It's a survival mechanism. But what if, at that pace, we miss an opportunity right under our noses? *Survive* is the *only* thing we are trying to do. We've been successful, but only because we look at the person next to us, size him up, decide if we are doing better or worse, and then carry on. It's a very sloppy operating procedure. There is a better way.

Your brain weighs about 2 percent of your body weight but consumes 20 percent of its energy. Most of that energy is a waste. Your brain is an energy hog. Yes, I said it. And now you know. That information has entered your brain, and now you'll think about it and waste some more energy doing so. You'll come up with opinions and ideas, get defensive about what your thoughts are and how they are meaningful, and then remember that you didn't call your mom back. You'll feel hungry, and realize you've been sitting still for too long and your butt hurts, and, oh yeah, you need to start on that diet, and why did your boss give you a funny look today, and on and on.

You have about 70,000 thoughts per day. Your mind is spinning relentlessly. Ninety-eight percent of the thoughts you had yesterday are the same ones you had the day before. That's why Monday looks like Tuesday, and June of this year looks like June of last year, which probably wasn't much different from June the year before that.

Your mind is always busy creating thoughts—the vast majority of which are on autopilot. The 'thinking mind' takes up a lot of energy talking to itself. That's not *you* talking to *you*. It's just the part of the brain that uses language. It wants—*needs*—something to do (or so we have come to believe). It is the beginning of where we've gone wrong. We think too much, and it has destroyed our ability to focus. Letting go of those endless thought loops is the single most important skill you will gain.

For every interruption, it takes your brain twenty-five minutes to re-engage fully. We are interrupted, on average, every forty seconds when in front of a computer and every 10 minutes in daily life. You can do the math if you like, but I think you can pretty quickly tell that we aren't very engaged.

Talking to yourself can be a great way to solve problems but doing it all the time is like sitting in your car in neutral with your foot on the gas pedal. Many people who are suffering from depression know this very well. They'll tell you, "I think too much." The mind is trying desperately to solve problems, most of which are unsolvable. It can be something as innocuous as 'why did that car cut me off', or something more life altering; 'why didn't I get the job', or deeper tragedies "why did my loved one have to die". We may never know the answers to many life questions and dwelling on them only prolongs the pain and opens the door to new problems. We come up with answers to feel at peace because apparently, some solution is better than no solution. And if we can't find a solution, the wheels will spin indefinitely in an endless loop— and that's what the mind ends up spending its time doing. You're never going to know why that car cut you off and concluding that you didn't get the job because you're too young, or not educated enough, is a silly conclusion that may make you feel better, (kinda), but it's not the real *why*. The tougher life questions are where we are the most vulnerable. You may be searching desperately for reasons why you lost a loved one but coming to the wrong conclusion will prolong the pain. It's a non-truth, and that keeps pain from dissipating. It's better to feel your way through the pain, without searching for a reason.

What if you stopped doing all that and only used your brain to solve problems that *do* have a solution? Not problems like, "What should I eat?" but more significant issues like, "How can we clean the world's oceans?" What if you only put your foot on the gas pedal when the car was in gear? How much gas do you think you'd save?

It's okay not to solve something. Get in the habit of knowing that **not knowing** is okay.

The 'talking mind' is a very, very, very small fraction of *you*, like the tip of the iceberg. Let's say the part of your mind that you call *'you'* is the tip of the iceberg that's sticking out of the water, the part that's talking and answering. It does the analytical thinking. It does the problem-solving. It uses words and language. It forms opinions and tells other parts of the mind and body when and to what degree to use emotion.

Now imagine the iceberg below. A real iceberg is 12 percent above and 88 percent below. To get a better idea of the actual scale of this 'talking mind' compared to the real you, imagine the distance from Los Angeles to New York. It takes 40 hours to drive. You will cross many states, many different towns, cities and mountains, and deserts. You'll get excited about the journey; you'll get bored, hungry, happy, contemplative, sad, sentimental, and on and on.

Now imagine the distance from Earth to the Moon. It would take about five months at 60 miles per hour, non-stop. This does not include stops at passing asteroids for photo ops.

Driving across the solar system would take about 810,000 years, assuming you don't have to stop for gas and stretch your legs.

This is the scale I'm talking about. The drive from Los Angeles to New York is the part that you think is 'you,' but in reality, it is more like the distance across the entire solar system. You think the short trip is you because it's the part of you that talks to you.

This idea is just conjecture, but I'm trying to show you the potential difference. There are as many neurons firing in your brain as there are stars in the Universe, but your 'talking brain' (the part that you think is all of you) is that very small fraction—the tip of the iceberg. The ratio of what you think is 'you' to what is really *you* is incomprehensible.

There are as many potential neuron connections in your brain as there are particles in the known universe. That is a lot of connections! To keep all the data your brain processes, it has a very ingenious way of saving energy. Your brain fills in a lot of gaps to give you a picture of the world that makes some sense. Your 'thinking brain' cannot possibly absorb all the data there is to process, so it takes shortcuts and gives you summaries. Your eyes, for example, have a large blind spot in them. The corneal nerve connects to the back of the eyeball directly in the center. Consequently, no rod or cone cells allow you to see what is directly in front of you. Your brain makes up the difference. It interprets what it believes is there by gathering data from the rest of your field of vision. Your eyes dart back and forth, and your head moves slightly left and right, and up and down, and each time the brain picks up more data until it fills that blind spot while simultaneously pulling from its memory to fill in the void. It knows from experience what Aunt Edna looks like, so it fills in the blind spot and recreates her nose when you cannot see it.

Even memories change over time to suit your mood or beliefs. They are not at all computer-like. Do you know that if you pull up old memories of a tragic event when you are happy, you will refile them as a happy event, and the horrible parts may fade altogether?

Five people that witness a crime 'see' different things and even those memories change over time. We are fallible, and we change our minds all the time but make up creative excuses as to why. We justify ourselves endlessly.

As fallible as memory is, we cling to it as if it was an integral part of us. Memories shape us, and we shape them. It's a constant shuffling of energy, and a lot of energy is lost in the process.

I'm asking you to let go of your bond with your memories. They are no more critical to today than an old movie you saw 20 years ago. I have nothing against memories. Take the lessons from them and move on, but keep in mind that the lessons you learned are from that past situation. That situation will never occur again the same way. Learn to play with your memories the same way you might rewrite a rough draft of a book.

Remember my analogy of the human eye not being able to see what is directly in front of you. Your mind is making up what is not there. It's doing the same thing to the memories you hold so dearly, and it doesn't bother to tell you. Remember that the part of you that you think is you, the 'talking to yourself' part of your brain, is a tiny part of you. The entire *you* is vastly more powerful, and a lot happens without you ever *knowing* about it.

You'll become more and more aware of those hidden happenings when you increase your skills, and eventually, you can manipulate them to accelerate your growth. Until then, here's a little tip to free up some of your brain power: make up your mind in the moment, or even better, just let go and don't make a decision at all. Otherwise, you're carrying the decision around with you. Over time, those decisions build up like sediment and slow down your ability to think and act.

You need to change how you think and then stop thinking altogether. Much—if not all—of the trouble you are having is because of how we have evolved. We're very social creatures and have an innate need to be accepted. We have an even stranger habit of talking to ourselves as if there was someone in our head with us. But the most damaging habit we have is our insatiable need to solve problems—or, at least, to feel like we have. We need closure. But why?

THE PROBLEM WITH BEING HUMAN

To keep from being lost, you look for landmarks relative to where you are.

You know you're here because the wall is four feet to your left and the door is ten feet to your right. Your position is relative to those things about you. We do this instinctively to find out *where* we are, but we incorrectly also do this to find out *who* we are.

You think you know who you are because you say that the man next to you is overweight, or he looks like your uncle John, or he looks wealthy, or he's nice—these qualifications are relative to other people that you've met before and relative to yourself. This is solely a comparative analysis. We define ourselves by evaluating others.

The weak-minded do this to make themselves feel better. We find solace in that we further understand ourselves and we're better than our peers. This is a false understanding. Calling that man fat doesn't make you skinny, and it doesn't give you a better understanding of who you are—it only denigrates your fellow human beings.

We define most things in our lives by comparing them to something familiar. When you describe something to a friend that he's never experienced, you find something to compare it to: "It tastes like a pear but has the texture of a banana."

You can see this fall apart in your world if someone calls you fat, idiot, poor, etc. It doesn't matter if it's true or not. If you're offended and you believe this person's evaluation, then he's got you. He owns you now. Those who truly know who they are never need to evaluate others or believe the evaluations of others. They exude unmistakable and unshakeable confidence. If you truly know yourself, you can never be offended. However, you can't honestly know yourself if you depend on your memories and past decisions because you've probably changed them to make yourself *right*.

We, as a species, have this tangled mess. We define ourselves by the decisions we've made from fallible memories, and we become upset if someone else's evaluation of us is not in alignment with what we have decided about ourselves.

You can never truly find yourself by comparing yourself to others—or, more importantly, by believing other people's evaluation of you. It's simply not possible.

You are you, and that is the simplest of truths. Defining who you are by comparing yourself to others is separating yourself from the people around you. You say he is X and that makes you Y. In reality, he is more like you than not.

As a species, we also falsely identify ourselves with things: I'm a man, I'm from Ohio, I went to art school, I am an American, I'm tired, I'm hungry, I'm friendly. These are all things that you're identifying yourself as. You link yourself to many different things and feel bonded to them as if these things were really you. When something contradicts that belief system, all of those carefully laid links get disrupted.

You might identify yourself as a well-educated man or a compassion-ate woman that always does the right thing. When someone calls you a jackass and cuts you off on the freeway, you get defensive because you think of yourself as a friendly, easy-going driver. Your image of yourself has been disrupted.

What if you made no such identifications? What if there were no such links in your mind? Think of that for a moment. Feel the peace that ensues.

It is possible to *know who you are* in the highest sense of the word. You can be *you* without comparing yourself to others and without belittling them. The only way to find this *knowing* is to stop comparing yourself to others and to stop believing what others say about you, good or bad. You are just you. That's all.

The decision and why positive thinking doesn't always work

It's a fairly common mantra to say, "Life is a culmination of the deci-sions you make." It is entirely accurate. Your state of affairs, where and how you live, what others think of you, and even your destiny are all based on the decisions you've made and are making. But what if you want to change the course of your life? Perhaps you're stuck in 'maybe.' Perhaps you simply aren't happy. You may hear things like, "Just be positive," "Imagine the future you want, and it's yours." There is a better way.

Consider this: you make decisions every waking moment (and maybe every sleeping moment). You decide what to wear in the morning, what to have for breakfast, when to tap your brakes and when to stomp on them. Countless decisions.

There are two types of decisions: Objective and Subjective.

Objective decisions are precise and have no real longevity. You make them and act on them, and it's done.

I'm leaving now. I'm watching TV. I don't like the neighbor's dog barking.

Subjective decisions are a little vague and don't have an end. They stick and pile up over time.

I hate Mondays. I can't believe it. I'm happy. I love dogs. I never have enough money.

Objective: *I am loving my dog Fluffy right now.* Subjective: *I love dogs.*

Neither is bad or good, just know that subjective decisions stay with you. You hold on to them. There is no time in them. They last until you make a contradictory decision.

You're making thousands of decisions every day. Over time, they become generalized. The "I hate" and the "I can't" start to form your opinions about other things, which is a basis for new decisions.

One day, you wake up and decide to "think positive" to make your life a little nicer—but you lose interest by lunchtime.

Subjective decisions accumulate like sediment in the forest. Leaves fall to the ground, pile up, compress, turn to dirt. More leaves and debris fall, and the pressure turns the bottom layers to stone. You see this in older people getting set in their ways.

There are a couple of solutions. The first is to make enough new decisions in the opposite direction (hopefully positive) to counter-act the sheer weight of your past decisions. The second solution is to take the more precise route of finding (remembering) the exact moment you made the decision.

Example: Joe, at the age of thirty, has hated dogs for as long as he can remember. He can either "think positive" about dogs for as long as it takes to counteract three decades of adverse decisions about dogs *or* find the memory of the first time he decided he hated dogs.

He might find that he hated the neighbor's dog after it bit him as a boy. Spotting that exact moment gives that decision an anchor in time, so to speak, and allows him to make a *new* decision not based on past experiences.

That mechanism is one of the most common reasons a person is held back in life. A person's general decisions get compacted so thoroughly it's impossible to "think positive" about it. He gets stuck in fixed ideas.

This small change in your thinking will help immensely. If you're going to make a decision, make it precise with some end point. When pos-sible, don't make a decision at all about a situation.

"I hate *this* Monday," although negative, is much better than "I hate Mondays." The best solution, however, is to not make a decision about Monday. It is a pure waste of mental energy. The latter will compound, and then you're destined to have bad Mondays for eternity. Ugh.

THE JOURNEY

Imagine for a moment a teenager. He's very thoughtful. He thinks his way through situations and considers all points of view. He's wants to know and understand things. He questions what he sees and what he's told. He's really fascinated by the capabilities of the mind and humankind. Although in his young mind it's not very well defined, he has the idea that there was something more magnificent than what we perceive with our senses. He wants to be able to walk into any situation without fear or apprehension and sees no reason why it couldn't be that way.

If *someone* could do something extraordinary, why not *everyone* and at *any time*? This idea starts simply. He'd go to an amusement park with his family and be terrified to go on roller coasters—but something didn't make sense to him. Other people could go on it and not die. He'd sit and watch them. He has proof. He calculates the numbers in his head. The vast majority are even smiling and having fun. Why is he terrified? He has no reason to believe it is dangerous. Maybe there's something buried in a deeper memory that he has consciously forgotten, but it's still affecting him. What if he had a near death experience when he was very young?

He was about 5 years old, and a traveling carnival was in town. The safety standards are pretty low, but as a kid, concerns of that caliber never enter his young mind. He and his friend climb onto the first ride they find. It's the Octopus, or sometimes called the Sizzler. It goes round and round, and each arm had several arms that spin on a smaller axis. He and his friend are too little for the ride. Everything starts out fine, but as the centripetal force builds, their small frame bodies are pushed against the side. The safety bar, if you can call it that, is made for adults, and they simply slide down under it and are forced down to where your feet should be. They're now out of sight and as the ride spins around, it looks like nothing more than an empty seat. A few more moments and they'll be thrown under the ride and hit but the other spinning cars.

The boy's mom doesn't see her son anymore and screams "STOP!" The man operating the ride sees nothing wrong and no reason to stop the ride. He stops it anyway; in case the screaming lady was right.

In this scenario nothing terrible happens, but the mind took in everything and doesn't forget, ever. The near-death experience places a lasting impression, so that many years later a generalized fear of amusement park rides still lingers.

Now, standing in front of a roller coaster many years later, the young teenager has no conscious memory of the Octopus ride. There he stands, frozen in deep thought trying to understand the illogicalness of fear. His family is not pushing him, but he knows he's not going to get on that thing. Then it hits him. There's some connections going on in his brain. He's pulling up some of the memory, not the event, but the decisions he made at the time. It was a one in a million incident and nothing bad actually happened, and since then he's never known of anyone to ever be hurt on a ride. He reaches some deeper understanding about life. There is *something* about the decisions we make that alter the course of our lives. We have an insatiable desire to conclude, right or wrong, and then that's it. We have decided. We put that decision to rest, and it becomes part of us.

He, at that moment, makes a new decision. Fear is not logical—it's like a cloud that surrounds you and inhibits thinking. It is merely a lack of data, and fear fills that void. Your mind hates a vacuum. It wants to know and understand. It's how we jumped up the evolutionary chain: solving problems, or, at least, wanting to feel like we are.

When there is no data, that void must be filled with something, and that something is fear of the unknown. In an attempt to get past that fear, our minds spin, and we talk to ourselves in never-ending cycles until we sort out some *solution*. Whether or not that *solution* will help is not relevant. Our brains simply want to stop thinking about it, but it has to *feel* like it has come to a conclusion.

When you come into a new situation, you are made aware that there's something you have no information for, and the mind moves into an unknown. Your mind will fill that void with irrelevant data or real data and sort through what it needs. Otherwise, it will spin endlessly, searching for a solution that will never come. This is where indecision starts, which is a precursor to depression. It's the fear of the unknown that causes you to sit on the couch when you should be doing something more meaningful. I use the word *fear* very loosely. I don't mean that you're afraid, necessarily, but your thinking mind has shut down while the rest of you is in a sort of void while trying to process what *might* happen.

There are two things at play here: attachment to past decisions and an unknown future. You are sitting on millions of past decisions and opinions, and you don't know what will happen in the next 20 minutes, let alone the next 20 hours or 20 years.

Nothing is holding you back besides the things that you have already decided. The "I can't," or "I'll get hurt," or even the sneakier, "I just don't feel like it." *And*, when you can't decide, your mind spins endlessly, looking for a solution—and wasting more energy in the process. You can do anything. You can solve any problem. But you have to learn the secret and trust it.

You get bogged down while your mind is trying to estimate what the next few minutes will be like from the trillions of bits of data it has. Both of these issues, working in tandem, are the basis for an ordinary, mainstream life. After giving you more information, I'll give you the solution that will set you free.

It is speculated that as the brain was evolving in early homo sapiens, they had the idea that there were ghosts, spirits, or gods in their heads talking to them. There would have been a point in our evolution when language was developing, and early man would be speaking out loud to his tribe. One day, someone realized he could talk to himself internally. Can you imagine the surprise? He'd look around wondering who was speaking to him and if anyone else heard it. How many people are in that little space you call a skull? It's a strange concept to imagine but has very profound implications.

As adults, we think it's sort of cute that kids have imaginary friends. We believe it's innocently silly, but for a while, it was decided in psychology circles that children should be dissuaded from doing so, as it was clearly *'insane'*. It's much more likely that their brains were growing into that phase when they start talking to themselves. They simply made that 'new voice' a friend. We still do it as adults, but we think of that voice as 'me.' Unless, of course, you do it out loud. Then you *are* 'insane.' I mean that to be facetious and a little humorous. So many of the opinions we throw around are not based on anything in particular.

We now have evolved to talk to ourselves all the time. We have conversations with ourselves. It's *normal*, but it's a massive waste of energy. This is why meditation is so beneficial. You can easily find tons of research explaining the benefits of meditation. Still, the simplicity is that you stop using your thinking brain to jibber-jabber to yourself, that mental energy is not being used up, and you feel peaceful.

Meditation rituals ask you to watch your breath—to concentrate on it. This is an excellent method to a point. When you stop talking to yourself and slow down your mind, it's your breathing that you start to notice. That's probably how this tool came about. For meditation, it's a good thing to focus on because it's much less 'noticing' than you were doing before, but it's still a stopping point. It's the last thing you notice before you stop thinking altogether. When you're about to drop off into the field, I'm trying to get you into, watching your breath is the last thread you hold on to before letting go. Let go.

This is mere conjecture on my part, but I imagine it's also why music, television, movies, the Internet, and social media are so popular. These things give your mind a break from talking to itself. How in-depth is your self-talk when you're listening to your favorite '80s rock? It'll keep your mind from spinning. It's less effective than just keeping your mind silent, but it's an excellent way to calm it down.

It is, however, still a significant drain on the mind. Your mind is still processing *all* of that data: every note, every word, every instrument, every pluck of every guitar, every emotion that you are reminded of. The time you couldn't get up the nerve to ask the pretty girl to dance or the ballad that you played over and over again when *she* broke your heart is all connected to the music of your past.

You should only be using that part of your brain to solve problems—and when you fine-tune this muscle, you can solve any problem in moments.

Once in a while, when you need to solve a problem or get something done, you engage your mind; it drops into gear with a thud—and you're off. This is opposed to having it always in gear and fully revved up all the time. That is what is wearing you out.

I mentioned imaginary friends earlier and how, as homo sapiens evolved, there was a point where we heard voices in our heads—which was a part of us. I suspect this is where our concept of God came from. Why is the high priestess the High Priestess? Because the gods talk to her? Why not me? Did Joan of Arc hear God speaking to her, telling her to defeat the English? What did God have against the English? Maybe she was experiencing the same thing that kids do when they have an imaginary friend, but instead of her friend being 'Billy,' hers was God?

Two people hear a voice in their heads. One concludes that it's merely him talking to himself. The other concludes that it's not himself but some unknown and all-knowing force. It's not a big stretch. I'm not suggesting there isn't some grand force that created the Universe. Still, I am suggesting that our interpretation of the evolutionary tool we were given of being able to talk to ourselves has been interpreted differently by different people.

Maybe that voice is God, and in that case, you are vastly more powerful than you give yourself credit for. A little goal like improving everyone's lives on the planet should be pretty easy, and that is what I'm teaching you to be ready for. Quite frankly, you *are* that person.

Why was Joan of Arc's voice God, and yours is just you? Did God talk to Moses, or was Moses talking to Moses? I love and respect these historical figures. I love what they've done for you and me and our history. I only bring this up to point out that you have everything they did, except you have more information and a greater understanding of how the mind works—and how freaky powerful you are.

What happens to consciousness when you stop talking to yourself? "I think; therefore, I am." What if you stop thinking? This is where all other creatures are. They're not using language to talk to themselves. They are just feeling—but by our definition of consciousness, we no longer have it without language. Consciousness is the ability to realize that you are watching yourself think about something while you're thinking about something, but that doesn't happen when you're not talking to yourself. You are simply being there. It's very peaceful. It opens the door to feel any feeling you want.

The difficulty many people have is that they get stuck in emotional states. When you're sad and can't get out of it, it's depression. There's very little energy available, not even enough to break free of those bonds. Even being stuck as happy all the time, is a bit insane. When you give your mind more space to handle incoming emotions it has room to pivot. You're not pinned down and trapped in one emotion. You can feel happy simply by deciding to be that way. All emotions are much more fluid. You can be happy all the time, but the difference is that it's a choice. You can also decide to be sad over something, but just as easily snap out of it and try something else. The upside is that you become much more efficient if you're not weighed down by the emotion that life has drilled into you. You have a freedom to do as you please and feel the way you'd like to. Do you want to get overly excited about an icecream cone, or break down sobbing over a sad love story, let those emotions fly—you can and should have that choice.

When you give yourself more mental capacity by not thinking so much, your mind opens up. It becomes receptive to the rest of the Universe. Solving problems takes minutes. You don't even have problems—you have solutions. Poof! No more problem. Having problems is just a consideration you carry around with you, anyway. You don't need it. It creates drama. Homo sapiens have a silly desire to always have something to do. Doing nothing is often more rewarding.

My hope is that eventually, something clicks in you. You have always had that burning fire to create something of great importance. I'm here now, calling back to you from your future, telling you that you pulled it off. Your momentum will increase slowly at first, but you become a true force. It gets easier as you get more done, and you start to realize the real power you have.

If the most extraordinary people throughout history had a voice in their heads that they called God and accomplished great things because of it, perhaps it was a misinterpretation of the mind simply talking to itself. Or maybe it really was God. It doesn't matter—you have the same ability and desire that all of them had, and perhaps more.

You now know that the voice in your head is a very, very small part of you. The use of language is simply a condensation of ideas and concepts, at least when it's used efficiently. When you talk to yourself, it's a feeble attempt to sort out problems or simply keep busy out of habit, but it's a massive waste of energy, and consequently, so are all negative emotions. As you become more efficient with this new way of being, you'll see problems fade away. You won't get sick—ever. You'll always be on top of your game. You'll never have a bad day—ever! Life will become a joy, not a struggle to survive. Then you'll start to look for a new, bigger game, which will impact all of us.

What if you were at peace, and your mind was quiet? What if you weren't talking to yourself but you were just being there, silent, not using language to sort through stuff. "What should I wear to work tomorrow?" "Why did that driver flip me off?" "Why am I hungry when I just ate?" What if you were just sitting there, relaxing—not having relaxing thoughts, but simply not thinking with words?

There is an analogy that is often used in self-help books about sledding down a hill. If you go down a hill a few times, a path starts to form. The more you go down the hill, the more likely you are to take the same path. Each passing compresses the snow a little more until the sled rudders need a lot more energy to jump the tracks, so you continue on the same trajectory. Each time your brain executes an action or has the same thought, you are more likely to take the same path you did the last time. It is suggested that you alter that path a little each time to keep the mind active. That's a great start, but the end goal here—and I must stress this—is to move well beyond simply making changes to better your life. If you are to reach the state I know you can, it would help if you didn't go down that hill at all. I'm asking you to move *up* to a higher plane of existence. Don't go down that hill. I'm asking something much bigger of you. I'm asking you to stop trying to be you. I'm asking you to exist. The magic happens here, and it is effortless and beautiful.

PROBLEM-SOLVING AND YOUR HAPPINESS

We have an insatiable need to solve problems and to have problems in the first place.

It's never a good idea to, "Just walk away from your problems."

That's a bad idea. It's easier and more beneficial to "Walk away" or "Let go" *after* solving the problem. It's human nature to solve problems, and it's challenging to let go of an unsolved problem. Walking away relieves you of the symptoms, but the problem doesn't get solved. Solving problems takes practice. You get better at it by digging in and rolling up your sleeves. It makes you a better person and builds character.

Getting in the habit of walking away creates a troubled person who will find life a struggle. Even small life issues become overwhelming. This is especially true in personal relationships, which is a huge factor in anyone's happiness, as it has the most unknowns.

Solving problems by taking drugs, illegal or psychiatric, is the same as walking away. It's not confronting the real issue. Your boss fired you, so you go have a beer—will that get you a new job? You're so depressed you take a drug to help you cope. It didn't solve your problem; you're just a little less alive. The solution is to find more data and getting your mind to work more efficiently.

That being said, I'm not suggesting that you shouldn't walk away from a dangerous relationship or situation. Sometimes the problem is bigger than your capability to handle it. Problem solving, after all, takes practice. Even in school, you learn numbers, then math, algebra, geometry, then calculus. With enough practice, you're a rocket scientist—little steps. Skipping to the most challenging problems would throw you into chaos.

If you're having trouble solving a problem, the single biggest reason is simply missing data. You've heard the adage, "A good relationship takes good communication." That's only half the answer. The goal of communication has to be to solve problems. It needs that purpose. It's data gathering that's then used to solve problems. This is the goal of communication. Talking is **not** communication. Arguing is **not** communication. Communication is asking good questions to gather data and use that data to solve a problem. That *problem* could be as simple as caring about someone and wanting to know how their day went so you feel closer to them, or it could be solving the problem of 'why don't you ever take out the trash?' Objectively asking for data is much more useful than creating turbulence with an argument to solve your problem.

Also, keep in mind that the wrong solution is apparent for the simple reason that the problem still exists. That seems obvious, but if you've ever had a problem that won't seem to go away, that's the culprit. If yelling at your kids doesn't get them to behave, stop doing it. It's not working. Try something else. If getting drunk every night isn't solving your problems, stop doing it. It's not working. Try something else.

Everything you do should be solving a problem. You get hungry, you eat. Problem solved. If you eat when you're not hungry, you're not solving a problem—you're creating a new problem. **This is extremely important.** If you are ever going to get to an enlightened state, you're going to have to push this idea to its extreme. Everything you do should be solving a problem: every action, every thought, *everything* that you are responsible for.

Get in the habit of evaluating your every thought and action. Is what you're doing or thinking right this instant solving a problem? Relaxing on the couch solves a problem if you're tired, but if you've been sitting there for two hours and you've got work to do, your solution is now the problem.

This takes a lot of practice. The goal is to undo how you've grown up and how you've been raised—not just by your family, but by society. We are social creatures—overly so. We want to be like people we perceive as successful, but we only see the outside. What happens in that space we call a skull is the *only* thing that matters. We simply don't know how happy that pretty girl on Instagram is or how happy that guy driving his Lamborghini is. You'll never know. Stop talking to yourself about it. It's a waste of mental energy. There is no feedback.

Feedback is so essential in improving any situation. You're trying to learn to play the piano, but you are deaf. How difficult would this be? There is no auditory feedback. You are on your own. You might just go for it—this is best—but society cringes at the sounds. We have evolved with the wrong feedback. Looking at others to see how we should be is giving us a false picture. Even if it were accurate, you have no real way of knowing. Others look to you to see what is acceptable while you're looking at them. This method only works to a certain degree.

It works as civilization evolves—we are here after all, and we've accomplished a lot—but we're looking at how green the neighbor's lawn is instead of pursuing our childhood dream of becoming an artist, or an astronaut. We have no feedback on 'happy.' I'm here to tell you that *happiness* is a decision, and it has nothing to do with what you tell yourself—*nothing*. It has nothing to do with language or words. You *feel* happy. You can start now if you wish.

I know this sounds weird, so maybe an example is in order. Lets say you have a pet dog. You are very bonded. You rescued him from the dog pound, and you suspect he's had a tough life. He knows you saved him. You look at your dog and say the words, "I love you," and feel them. He looks back at you with those big brown eyes, and he **only** *feels* **the emotion**. He's not thinking, "I love you, too." He is only feeling it. For all we know, he's doing this with the entirety of his soul. His brain is focusing on you, and he's absorbing all the inputs. His eyes are locked on you, he smells you, he hears your voice, he's feeling your hands around his face. How much energy do you think he's using, even though he's not using language? He is *all in*.

I'm teaching you how to be like this with everything you do. I imagine, in your current state, that when I say, "all in," you're thinking you'll need to roll up your sleeves and really put a lot of effort into it—but it's the opposite. It is without any effort, and that's the key. You're already putting too much effort in, and it's nearly all wasted.

How much effort do you think the brain uses to convert 'I love you' into words? It takes a lot, and you don't realize it because that's all you do. You convert things into words. Are you tired at the end of the day? It's because you spent the entire day talking to yourself. It's weird to say, I know. I get it.

Decisions don't take language. They don't take words. They only take intention. Feelings are the same way.

I think we have gone off the rails as a species. We have over complicated things with our addiction to thinking—to talking to ourselves.

When you look into your dog's eyes, and say the words to yourself, "I love you, buddy," it takes a certain amount of effort to process those words into a sentence, tell them to yourself, and then you may feel that love to some degree. We've been saying things with words so long that we have long since forgotten there is a pathway from a much more intense feeling—from an emotion.

When your dog looks back at you—he *only feels the emotion*. Nothing more, nothing less. There's no convolution, no thinking, no deciding what that means, no qualifying it into something less, like "I'd love you more if you'd give me a cookie." It is pure love.

We mistakenly say, "I'm going to make a million dollars," but we leave out the intent. Language without intent is simply words without meaning. If you want to make a million dollars, *feel* like making a million dollars. Saying the words is entirely secondary, even unnecessary.

A dog sees a squirrel. He doesn't say to himself, "I'm going to go get that squirrel." He only has the intention that people would describe in words such as "Get squirrel". His intention is vastly more than our words.

Words are a *very* watered-down version of what is intended.

Try it for yourself. Look at your husband or wife, kids, or pets. Look them deeply in the eyes and feel love for them, without using the words "I love you."

The intent is everything. You cannot fail if you hold on to your intention. The stronger it is, the less conflict you have in your world, the more effective it is. If you have a firm intention, problems have no space to creep in. They don't have any room in your head. When you get to this state, a simple, effortless intention becomes a reality. But you'll never see this happen if you clog your mind with unnecessary decisions, opinions, and spinning thoughts.

Talking to yourself is okay to work through a problem, but I'm betting you'd never have had the problem if you had stopped talking yourself into one. You'd just cut to the chase in everything in your life. You'd move with intention, and problems would have no time to form.

Depression and mental illnesses are an epidemic in our society. I believe this will become the biggest problem we have ever faced—and it is caused by language, talking to ourselves too much, and accepting the opinions of others and ourselves.

You've often heard the phrase, "I'm thinking too much," or "I can't help thinking about it." Overthinking is a problem. I suggest any thinking (besides specifically solving a problem, which should only take a minute or so) is unnecessary. It is greatly therapeutic when you stop.

You are not the voice in your head. Your brain uses language to express emotions and thoughts. The voice in your head is a tool that you use. It is not you. You originate feelings, ideas, and dreams, and your brain organizes all that into words that make all of it more concise. However, your brain leaves out a lot of the "umph." It leaves out a tremendous amount of the "umph."

You can yell at your dog in an angry voice, "You're such a good dog. You're so good." Or the opposite. You can say, "You're such a bad dog," in a sweet, kind voice. He'll react to the intention, not the words. We've gotten overly hung up on the words and have lost the true gut feelings. A much more affluent and more straightforward life is a life free of being stuck in negative emotions. Language and self-talk keep someone stuck in negative emotions. Language is slow and sticky. Emotions, though intense, are much more fluid and can resolve quickly.

Have you ever had trouble finding the words to express how you feel? Words are a relatively new thing to homo sapiens.

Learn to feel what you're feeling without words. Practice not talking to yourself all the time. It's very liberating.

OUR NEED TO SOLVE PROBLEMS

Never, ever cause a problem—for yourself or anyone else. It isn't possible, but it is the goal. If you're not solving a problem, you are causing one. The net result of your solution has to be an improvement in the Universe. Not just for you and your family, or your business, or your country. Not even for all humankind, or all living things, or all nature, but *everything*. Stealing your neighbor's lawn ornaments will make *your* lawn look nicer, but...

For better or worse, we got to where we are because of our insatiable desire to solve problems. Having the right solution seems to be secondary to having *a solution*.

You are successful in life to the degree that you are indeed right, not just thinking you are right. Life lets you win a little more if you are truly right in your solutions. If you're wrong and you know it, that's actually being right.

If you're wrong and think you're right, life has a way of kicking you in the teeth. The guy that robs a bank is 'right' because "other people have more money than they deserve, and it's okay to take it from them."

We have been so groomed to be 'right' that we're missing our true potential. It's time for you to create the change for yourself and others by leading the way.

Many philosophies will tell you the ultimate goal is to get to a point where you 'know' everything. "It is the peak of existence." I believe that is wrong-headed. Peace is found in differentiating what you know from what you don't know. 'Maybe' is fine, as long as you know that you're in a 'maybe.'

In practical terms, this means to not jump to conclusions. Joe comes into your office for a moment and leaves. The next day, you realize your favorite pen is missing. As a human being with an insatiable need to solve problems, you solve this by concluding that Joe took your pen. You never confront him, but you treat him a little differently every time you see him. You may not even know you're doing this. The more alert and mindful you are, the more you'll see this happening. For the most part, it's still below your conscious awareness. He senses something different with you and has also come to a wrong conclusion. He thinks you hate him because he said "Hi" to your wife at the company picnic, and he imagines you think he was flirting with her. This phenomenon spirals on throughout your life (and his), causing untold problems never to be solved.

This phenomenon is a large part of what holds a person back in life. Wrong solutions are what breed a lack of confidence, as well as other phenomena that grow exponentially worse. The false data you gather and use to create who you are is based on many wrong assumptions—wrong or right, you'll never really know. The shortcut to this, the only way to defuse the situation, is to stop forming opinions about everything and ultimately stop talking to yourself—except to solve a particular problem. If a solution doesn't pop into your head immediately, you are simply missing data. Find the missing data, then confront the issue again.

Meanwhile, stop talking to yourself about the problem. Please keep in mind that the wrong solution can also pop into your head. Always ask yourself, objectively, once you have found a solution, "Is there any way this might not be true?" It's the litmus test to your conclusion. In the case where you concluded that Joe took your pen, you'd ask yourself, "Is there any way that something else happened besides Joe taking my pen?" If 'yes,' then explore those. You might look around and find your pen on the floor behind your desk. It's more likely that it rolled off your desk and fell—but even that is an assumption. Joe could have hidden it there. I mean that to be facetious. The point is that I want you to get how much mental energy you're spending on things that don't matter. You have your pen now; get to work on something meaningful that will have lasting results.

Any problem that has a correct solution will resolve immediately, without causing new problems. Agreeing that you don't know is a viable and real solution. It is a truth, and it will stop the above phenomena from spiraling. It's okay if you don't know where your pen went. The simple solution to this is to ask questions. Find the data that you are missing. It's such an easy thing to do, and yet many people simply don't do it. It may feel like you are hyper-critical of the other person or accusatory. Being mindful will help. Saying "Hey Joe, I can't find my favorite pen, can you help me find it?" is a lot better than "Where's my pen?" Even that is better than coming to a wrong conclusion that will affect your relationship from here on out.

We pick the easy answer, whether it's right or wrong. We decide that we can't get ahead in the world because we are of a certain race or gender, or too old, or too poor, or too serious, etc., but there's no real data to back that up for your particular situation. It becomes a reason, but not a solution. We pick the *easy reason* because we are lazy, and it takes a little more effort to get to the truth.

More importantly, it's that the unknown future makes us think a little harder. You have a favorite pen because there is less thinking or distractions to have one. This particular pen feels good in your hand, and the ink always flows nicely out of it, and you seem to write better with it. The truth is that it doesn't give you distractions, or you've created some opinions about it.

You have an intention in your head, conscious or otherwise. You're going to sit down, grab your favorite pen and write something. Simple. You haven't even verbalized this in your head. You have, to some degree, predicted your future on a subconscious level. The unknown future is the biggest obstacle we have, and it's what trips us up the most. You reach for your pen, and it's not there. If you had a lot of mental energy to spare, this wouldn't be a big deal. However, suppose you're already maxed out and don't have much mental capacity to spare. In that case, this disruption of your predicted future, which again is the biggest obstacle we have to our survival, is traumatic. You get mad over a very minute alteration to your predicted future.

You only find this troubling because it altered your perception of what your future should be. You intended to grab your favorite pen and use it; now it is gone. Because your mental energy is so embroiled in other things, this little diversion is unsurmountable, and you get stuck trying to solve an incredibly trivial issue. Stop having a *favorite pen*, grab any pen and get back to what you were doing. Create a future where you're the person that nothing seems to bother you, and you get all of your goals done!

This is your *intention versus reality* and it's what is frustrating about life. You are only upset with the guy that cut you off on the freeway because you had predicted yourself being in that lane in the next few milliseconds, and now that future is not possible.

When your mind is full of stuff, you don't have the mental capacity to adapt to sudden change. You need a buffer. If you don't have that buffer, you take the first solution that comes to mind. You feel some relief that you've arrived at some conclusion. It's not caused by having the *correct answer*, but by getting *some* answer.

Someone cuts you off on the freeway. "Idiot."

Problem solved.

He's an idiot; you're not. It's a simple solution, but the wrong one. It's okay not to know why he cut you off. Still, if you carry on solving that problem every time someone disrupts your intention, you'll eventually believe that everyone is an idiot. Their solution will be to treat *you* like an idiot.

Mindfulness and other self-help mantras will teach you to be aware that maybe he's just having a bad day, or he didn't see you. Other teachings will ask you to take complete responsibility for the act. "You shouldn't have been in his way," or some other nonsense. There is a much more efficient and effective way to go about it: Don't decide at all. Please don't talk to yourself about it. It was a non-event. Why do you need to feel better about it? Why do you feel bad in the first place? Another car moved in your direction for a brief moment in time—that is all. You tapped your brakes and carried on.

If you spend too much time in this phenomenon, it blocks your ability to genuinely observe the world around you. You become very busy being 'right.' Your intellect drops, your ability to communicate decreases, and life will become a burden.

Get good at solving problems and know, factually, that you have the right solution. Otherwise, realize that you don't know and move on to a more solvable problem. Like any skill, it takes practice.

Jumping to conclusions is an exercise in futility. Don't do it.

THE THINGS WE
TELL OURSELVES

We have become so accustomed to having an opinion; most assume you must have one. As far as the mind's efficiency is concerned, having an opinion is like pouring glue onto your keyboard. That may sound odd but hear me out. You don't need to have an opinion. Opinions are energy wasters. Do you like chocolate or vanilla? Everyone has a preference. Why is that? Does it matter? You decided a long time ago the answer to that question, and now, to conserve mental energy, you stay consistent because changing your mind will take more mental energy—or so you think. You, from then on, like chocolate and not vanilla. What if you never made up your mind, are served vanilla ice cream, and you sit there and enjoy (without words) the rich, cold, sweet feeling in your mouth? What if you simply enjoy life instead of making your mind up about it?

When you go out to eat, you always get a steak. You want it medium, and you insist on having a steak knife. The mashed potatoes should have a little divot in the middle where you will pour the gravy—you have to do it so it's just right. You like asparagus because the bitter taste perfectly accents the steak flavor. The dollop of butter you carefully put on top of the steak just before you cut off the next slice is the "only way to have steak." It's always red wine, Pinot Noir of a good year. You're not an expert, but your boss likes it, so you decide you like it, too. It's the only wine you've ever tried. This is what you're expecting while waiting for your meal to arrive. You've walked into the restaurant with a masterfully composed conglomeration of opinions of how this is going to play out.

Your steak arrives. It's well done. You have French fries, not mashed potatoes, and some green beans that came from a can. Your wine never arrived, and your water has a bug in it. How do you feel now?

What if you *only* used your mind to solve problems? How much energy do you think you would have? I'll give you the facts again: You create 70,000 thoughts a day. What to eat? Why did that driver cut you off? What should you say when you call her?

Did you know that you have already made up your mind before the words trickle into your head? Processing the words of your thoughts is prolonged. Did you know that your muscles tighten, and your blood pressure increases moments before you *decide* to get up off the couch? The real you, not the part that talks to yourself, already decided to get up. Then it gets the body ready, then it sends the words to the prefrontal cortex of your brain and converts that concept into the words "Get up off the couch." What if you could *unlearn* all of that wasted energy and more efficiently use your brain's power to solve some real problems—or enjoy life more, stop worrying, maybe achieve *greatness*?

What if it is possible to do the things you see in fiction movies? Maybe you could sit down at a piano and play Nikolai's *Flight of the Bumblebee*, unrehearsed, flawlessly. What if the only reason this seems impossible is that your mind is busy talking to itself, using an excessive amount of energy?

Maybe you could wake up one day and be so in tune with the Universe you could make everything go perfectly your way.

You may have tried thinking positively, that you'll get a parking place close to the store, and presto-magico, as soon as you drive around the corner a spot opens up.

But—what if the mind knew it was going to be there anyway? What if you even told yourself to be surprised, but it knew already? We spend so much mental energy processing words that the other senses get little attention. The younger you are, the more likely you'll still see these things and be fascinated by them. Adults still see but they are rare enough that it can seem unreal. I am pretty sure it happens to everyone, at some level. We call it serendipity.

A boy is walking down the sidewalk in small town where he has grown up. The streets are all in a grid, North/South streets, and East/West streets, all evenly spaced. He suddenly has the image of another boy who moved away years prior pop into his head. He didn't know him very well but knew his name: Dale. He was a little younger, so never had any classes with him, but close enough in age that he knew who he was and would see him in the halls and at recess. In a momentary flash he knew that he was about to run into him, even though he hadn't seen him in years. He had no reason to ever think of him again, let alone see him as he had moved away many years prior. He rounded a blind corner, and, sure enough, there he was, walking straight toward him about a hundred yards away. There are so many ways you could explain that—telepathy, intuition, happenstance, luck, a fluke, etc.

A man decides to go for a swim in the ocean, drops his keys in his pocket, and goes snorkeling. After a day of fun and sun, he went back to his car and realized his keys were gone. He searched up and down the footpath from the beach to where he was lying and then realized they must have fallen out while he was swimming. He went back into the water and looked for hours until the sun was starting to set. Disappointed, he was about to give up when he noticed a father and son snorkeling a hundred feet offshore. He shouted to them, "Have you seen my car keys?" The boy held up a car key. They had just found it that very moment.

The thinking brain operates at a very high level, but it's just a filter. It has an incredible amount of data to sift through and draw conclusions about, and we think we are this thinking brain. To us, it is all there is. We think from here, so it must be us. We recall memories from here, so it must be us. We talk to this thing as if it were our best friend. *"What would you like for dinner? I don't know. What would you like?"* It *is* you—but only a very, very small part of you.

The entire you is vastly deeper, more substantial, and all-knowing. I know this sounds mystical, but we have conveniently forgotten our true potentials. Perhaps we never knew. Regardless, I'm here now to show you.

What if the boy knew Dale was coming around that corner because he felt his electrical signature or even smelled him long before he could have possibly seen him? I'm not suggesting that he smelled bad, but everyone has some attributes that our heightened senses might pick up on if we weren't so *busy.* Have you ever had the feeling that someone was watching you, and then turned your head to see that someone was indeed staring directly at you? You felt his electrical signature. You picked up on it.

A man was taking his dog down to the beach. He's a very clingy dog. He's never more than a few feet from his owner, but today he did something extraordinary. As soon as they get out of the car to head toward the beach, the dog bolts. Thinking that this was kind of strange, the man just stands there, trying to comprehend what is happening. He watched him run away for a moment too long, all the while expecting him just to turn around and come back any second. He kept going.

He started to run after him. He ran for about a half-mile. Then he could see, way off in the distance, a dead sea-lion on the beach. His dog knew it was something he needed to get close to from over a half-mile away. His nose knew. There's a vast amount of data right in front of you that you are blind to. You can tap into that data pool if you learn to look for it. All the answers you seek are there, but they are hidden when you're busy trying to solve problems with only the data in your head, most of which you make up to pacify some unresolved issues.

Maybe a few minutes before the boy ran into Dale, he was the passenger in a car that drove by, and he saw him subconsciously, which triggered the memory of him, making his walking toward him a big coincidence, but not nearly as much as it first appeared. Or maybe he saw him earlier in the day, and his memory triggered an electrical signal that the boy picked up on: "Dale is thinking of me, and he's close by."

We walk around talking to ourselves, and we miss all these extraordinary abilities we have. We waste all our energy on irrational thoughts, opinions, and problems.

The next time you go out to eat with family and friends, don't put any thought into what to order. Don't look at the menu. Just skim over it rapidly; point and say, "I'll have that." Takes about four seconds. Don't go into the restaurant with thoughts like, "I like fish. I don't like chicken. I'm in the mood for Italian." It's a waste of mental energy. To be honest, your body already knows what it needs. It'll crave what it wants 'you' to give it, and the thoughts it takes to express those things will be slow coming, so bypass all of that and know that if you just point to something and order it, it'll be okay.

If it turns out awful, don't form an opinion about it, just take the experience and move on. It's a hard habit to break, and I know some of the things I've said here will strike you as odd.

We are overly concerned about preventing things and having bad experiences. The odds of having a good or bad meal are incalculable. You can make an educated guess, but you would need more 'education' (data) to be 100 percent correct. Going to a restaurant and having a bad meal isn't enough data, so why are you spending so much mental energy over such a trivial thing?

The same goes for the things you decide about people. Evaluations you make of others stick with both you and them. Statistically speaking, you're probably wrong. Be very careful when you're evaluating someone.

We all do it. We have all gotten a little upset with someone and, to make ourselves feel better, evaluate the person so they're wrong and we are right.

We say, "She's a bitch," and "He's a jackass," and then we feel better—but that decision sticks, and it's probably not accurate. After all, you only chose that decision because it made *you* feel better.

But now, you treat that person that way, and he or she behaves that way because that's how you and others treat them, and so goes the downward spiral.

Now she's a bitch because you decided it, and you're a jackass because you treat her like a bitch.

Where does it end?!

Simple. Don't evaluate your fellow humans. It takes practice, but you'll end up appreciating the people around you much more, and they'll feel the same about you.

All of these decisions start to become habits that pile up and slow you down.

A great experiment conducted by Chabris and Simons illustrates my point beautifully. There's a video of two teams passing a basketball amongst themselves. Players run around in different directions, passing different basketballs among the various players. It's a little chaotic to watch. Viewers of the video are asked to count the number of times the White Team passes the ball.

The audience watches the video and does as instructed. Most get pretty close to the right number. Next, the audience is asked how many people saw the person dressed in a gorilla suit walk right through the entire scene, beat his chest, and then walk off-screen. Very few do, and those who did were more likely to have gotten the basketball pass count wrong. This is fascinating and proves how poor we are at concentrating and how much we miss. Once you master your mind by focusing all your mental energy by not forming unnecessary opinions, talking to yourself, or operating on fixed ideas, you learn to focus your mental strength and won't have this happen to you. You simply won't miss things. This is the basis of creativity and the core of your ability to survive in the world. You become more creative when you can connect ideas, concepts, and memories to form new things. You'll see the 'gorilla' that solves seemingly unsolvable problems.

HABITS

About 95 percent of everything you think and do is based on a habit. The mind uses habits as a way of conserving energy. You don't put much thought into brushing your teeth. It's so ingrained in your routine, and you just do it. Remember how awkward it was to tie your shoes when you were young? It takes quite a bit of hand/eye coordination, but now you can be talking to your dog about how fun the walk you're about to go on will be while he's jumping all over you, and also be thinking about what you'll have for dinner when you get home all while tying your shoelaces. Habits are how we can navigate our complicated world. Some of these habits are fine and even essential, but many keep you from evolving into something better. It's good for your mind to shake up all of your habits, whether they are fine the way they are or not. It keeps your mind limber. Brush your teeth with your non-dominant hand, or walk around your house backward, or sing your favorite songs with made-up lyrics.

Please don't try to break or disrupt all of your habits at once—you'll get overwhelmed. However, once you start breaking some old habits, it builds up that muscle, and the ability to break habits becomes a habit itself.

First, make a shortlist of habits you're aware of and pick one you'll work on. The overall goal is to break all the old habits that are holding you back, and more importantly, the ones that are holding you still. Some habits are obviously holding you back. Smoking would be a good one to tackle. Some are not harmful at the face, but they are preventing you from doing something more substantial. Turning on the news when you wake up in the morning may seem harmless, but what if you spent that time exercising instead? Imagine both scenarios if you did each for a year. How would each path deviate from the other? Take the course that is more in alignment with who you want to become.

As you start to tackle this, other habits will come to light. Things you never imagined you do will begin to surface. You might realize that you get a coffee every time you walk by the office coffee machine when you know full well you've had enough. Even getting tired at the same time every night is a habit. It's not necessarily bad, but your body knows when you go to bed, so when that time rolls around, the body's sleep chemical known as melatonin will kick in. Maybe you even have a habit of raising your voice in pitch when you talk to your boss, and she might see you as lacking confidence because she hears a high, sweet voice and surmises that you're not a go-getter. Higher pitched voices are more apologetic, kind, and sweeter. If you talk to a baby, you don't do it in your most resounding baritone. You'll start to become more aware of these things as you tackle this. Many habits are acceptable the way they are. Take a good, hard look at what it's doing to your future—mockup timelines for each that branch out in different directions. Then, write a little story about your future as you go down each separate path. Which path has the most significant benefit? You are going to go down one of these paths. Prime yourself now. Decide now so that it won't be a random choice or the wrong one.

As you start to drop these habits, you'll find that your ability to concentrate is heightened. This is probably the single most crucial skill you can gain. Focus!

Your mind drifting from random thought to random thought in a chain of weak links is the worst habit. It's often called monkey-mind. The best way to short circuit that pattern is to say what you're doing while you're doing it. Your mind drifts all over the place when you're doing activities, primarily if you are used to it. Instead, if you're washing the dishes, say, "I'm washing the dishes," over and over. It may seem silly, but it works. This reduces the thinking brain and forces you to do what you're doing while doing it. It's addicting once you push through the barriers. You'll find you get tasks done faster—*much faster.*

Imagine you're driving your car on the way to work. It's pretty easy to be thinking about what you will have to do at work when you get there, but I promise you'll be more efficient if you clear your mind while you're driving to work. When you get to work, set a timer to brainstorm what you need to get done that day. Pull off to the side of the road and do it then if you don't think it's possible to find the time when you arrive.

The analytical, talking part of your brain thinks, "Get up," then tells the body to do its thing, then the language brain turns all that into words: "I think I'll get up now." Regardless, all the fun stuff happens down below. Trust the subconscious. We don't give it nearly enough credit. It already runs the show—it may even be better at communication than 'we' are. Stop thinking in slow, methodical words and just do. Get a feeling, use your intuition, and move forward. It already runs your body. It beats your heart, moves your blood, pushes oxygen through your system, and digests your food. Millions and billions of actions are taking place, and you don't 'think' about them. The subconscious part of you has got those things wired. Let it do its job.

Habit Stacking

Link habits together. I have a habit of making coffee in the morning. Once it's made, my dog also has a habit of knowing he gets to go out. When we come back in, he gets fed, and when that's done, I review my finances, then exercise, then eat the same breakfast I had the day before. All of those habits are linked together into a chain. It's a good routine and very efficient. I don't think about it; I don't waste energy on "What should I do now?" I have rehearsed this. It's the same as yesterday. These are good habits.

I used to skip breakfast and not exercise (but want to). I'd have coffee, work through the day, skip lunch, go home tired and hungry, eat a huge meal, then fall asleep. One bad habit would lead to the next in a chain that lasted the entire day—and consequently, a lifetime.

That's a great example of habits that are all stacked together—one habit led into the next, and so on. It started with the bad habit of skipping breakfast, a meal when your brain needs protein and fat the most.

Schedule your time for anything you need to do daily. Make this a habit. It's a lot easier than setting weekly habits—in a week, and there's too much time in between. Exercise is a habit you need to do daily. Doing it once a week leaves too much time in between, and it's much too important. If you have trouble with this, start slowly. You simply must do it as soon as you wake up.

As a sidenote—we as humans create. We are all artists. An artist creates something from nothing. We create life, we produce things for work, we create laughter and happiness. We also create problems for ourselves and others. If you are embroiled in life's problems you need to create good things in greater abundance. If you are getting by in life, there's a balance between life's problems and what you are creating. If you want to raise the quality of your life, you simply need to tip the scales and create faster than life can present you with new problems. Be an artist.

Even feeling sad can be a habit. Maybe you feel sad every time you see a photo of your grandma that passed away years ago. It's a habit. You can just as easily feel joy every time you see the picture or think of her. One causes your body to kick in stress hormones that inhibit your thinking, productivity, and happiness. The other kicks in happiness hormones which make you more productive and peaceful with a quieter mind. Which do you think Grandma prefers you to be? Which would you choose to be?

Let's say you're down in the dumps. Life is bad for you. You're depressed, you hate your job, you're overweight, your spouse is always complaining about you and to you. You've learned to keep quiet. It is your baseline. You've become numb and don't spend much time on anything productive. Dreams are dead—you're just trying to make it through the day without getting fired. You've shut down.

You'd like to be wealthy suddenly, so you buy a lottery ticket every week. You know it's hopeless. Yet you still dream about it from time to time, not realizing that it drains you mentally. Your brain has even slowed down. There's not much going on up there. All you think is, "I don't want to be here; I want to be there."

You have to accept that you are where you are. It's one of those things that is hard to put into words. Words, again, just barely scrape the surface. We have become so conditioned to the idea that words express everything, but it's not as if saying the word "war" really describes the pain and suffering of entire cultures for decades. The *word* doesn't do war justice, nor do the handful of extra words I've feebly used to make my point. This is why people who can use words to convey an idea are highly rewarded for their talents—but even then, all the *umph* is missing.

You need to find a place where you can grow from. You grow when you're happy, but you *think* you can't be happy until you grow or move out of the place you're in.

Being grateful trains the mind to look for the good stuff in your life and gives you a place to launch your life from. There is also a much deeper and more meaningful reason to be grateful. Being grateful calms the mind; it's a shortcut. It takes your foot off the gas pedal and shuts the talking mind down. How much do you have to tell yourself when everything is going great? Have you ever heard someone complain about something? They can go on for a long time. There's a lot of energy there. When they are happy, that same person will say, "I'm great!" then sit quietly, smiling to themselves. Yet unhappiness spins the brain like a top.

Establish a base for yourself, and you can grow from that base. Imagine a seabird trying to take flight from rough seas. It's a horrible storm, pitch black. He's a seabird, but he's getting sea-sick; no food for days. He spreads his wings, launches with as much force as he can muster—and a wave clips his wings and throws his balance off. He nosedives into another wave, takes a gulp of water, and goes under.

Now imagine he launches with a full belly from the solid ground on a sunny day with a slight breeze. Reaction times are near instant—easy, fast, and efficient. This is the difference, as far as the mind is concerned. Even if you're in a bad spot in life, find the stable factors and be grateful. Gratitude is your base. "I'm grateful I'm free of that job; now I can find my dream job. I'm grateful I learned what not to say to my wife. I'm grateful that I'm a seabird and can witness the power of water." Gratitude calms the mind. It takes less energy to be grateful than it does to be worrisome and searching for solutions. Gratitude no longer takes your mental strength. You are done solving problems. Your mind stops endlessly spinning—why should it spin? You are grateful. Now you can launch a great future from that base.

We limit ourselves tremendously. We run our lives on a very thin horizontal plane of existence. From our viewpoint, the world is flat. We operate on that plane. It's a few thousand feet up and a few thousand feet down (into water). Even our solar system is flat. We naturally think in these planes: forward, backward, side to side—that's it. We're missing everything in between. Einstein so eloquently said, "We cannot solve our problems with the same thinking we used when we created them. This book's entirety attempts to get you outside of the *thinking mind* that you are stuck in, to see the whole picture rather than just what's right in front of you.

The Universe is mostly space—not only outer space, but the atoms in your fingernail are mostly space—and yet we concern ourselves with the little things we *can* see. It seems logical, but we are looking at the tip of the iceberg, the 0.00001 percent on the surface. The rest of the iceberg is unsolidified energy. It's malleable.

I'm asking you to stop limiting yourself.

If you *want* something, it tells your mind you are lacking. If you are grateful for what you have, then you have all you need. You are wealthy. Wealth is a mindset. Happiness is, too. People search for it, and yet it cannot be found outside of yourself.

I know you have greatness in you. There's a lot you need to do but I'm sure you can do it. There are many habits you need to break first—then you can get back on a track that will create what you are destined for. That burning desire deep inside you will not be wasted. Here's what you're going to do:

1. **Create a base with gratitude.** Your mind gets quiet when you are grateful. It allows you some extra mental energy to build a base that you can launch a better life from.

2. **Slow down your mind—conserve mental energy.** Start looking at how much you talk to yourself and think in terms of having a set amount of mental energy each day. It gets depleted as the day wears on and more quickly with heavy or constant thoughts.

3. **Reduce and eliminate distractions.** Look for and cut out any distractions in your life. Find the time of day you are most productive, schedule that time as your work time, and cut out any distractions.

4. **Habits, good and bad.** Become more cognizant of all your habits, systematically enforce the good ones, and eliminate the bad. Create a chain of good habits that will carry you throughout the day.

5. **Protect your vulnerable times.** You are most vulnerable when you first wake up, when you're about to fall asleep, when you're tired, and when you're hungry. Start and end your day with a positive goal or affirmation, take a nap if you're tired, and always have some food nearby. Don't make decisions when you're hungry or tired.

6. **Clean up memories.** Review your past and replace those memories with images of you being at your absolute best, then broadcast that image into what your future will be.

Doing these steps and mastering the techniques will significantly reduce the mental energy being wasted every day. Slowing down your spinning mind will be a giant leap forward for you. Our minds have a habit of constantly finding something to do. It thinks it needs to think, but it doesn't. Your mind is a motor that wants the gas pedal pressed down to the floor all the time, revving.

Just thinking, unless you are solving a specific problem, is a time and energy waster.

Getting better at this is the first real giant leap into new abilities and your greatness.

Start using your brain time more efficiently. When you need it, turn it on and use it for one specific purpose. Do A, then B, then C, and then shut it down. It's very concise and linear. The amount of extra time you'll have is staggering. You'll wonder what to do with yourself. Do not fall back into old habits. Learn a new language, play the guitar, become a chess master, solve world hunger. Challenge your mind.

The benefits of doing the steps above are limitless, but here are some things you can expect.

1. Much faster response time, both in reflexes and decisions.

2. Arriving at the correct solution and knowing that it is indeed correct.

3. Much healthier and rarely, if ever, sick.

4. More creative—you can pull from a vast data pool and make very obscure connections.

5. You become pan-determined as opposed to self-determined. Pan-determined means that your decisions are for the greater good, not just you.

6. You don't get worn out mentally.

7. You won't make careless blunders or make mistakes or get frustrated.

8. You stay happier and on an even keel. Others don't adversely affect you.

9. Goals are easily achieved.

10. You'll radiate peace, and others will be drawn to you—both good and bad people. Bad people will want to consume your energy, and Good people will adore you.

I do have to warn you of some things. You'll start to elevate yourself up and away from your peers. You'll begin to see more and more differences between who you are becoming, who you were, and where your peers are. Keep moving forward and upward. Bring good friends and acquaintances with you.

DISTRACTIONS

Turn off all notifications on your phone and computer. Don't answer your phone if you are concentrating on something. Your mind is taking in everything. Eliminate as much noise as you can.

Taking a walk in the woods is very therapeutic. Scientists have speculated that connecting with nature is perhaps the reason, but there are also fewer distractions. No electrical wires are humming, no traffic noises, no artificial lights. It's best to do this barefoot. Walk barefoot whenever you can. It's an excellent brain exercise, believe it or not. Your mind has to concentrate more intently when you walk barefoot. Balancing takes a lot of brain energy and doing it barefoot takes even more. You have to be involved in every action while walking barefoot, especially out in nature. Now that you are concentrating on every step, you aren't introverting. You are in a flow state. I would highly recommend this for people who are getting older. It has a nice side benefit in that it reconnects you with your mind and body. Also, the Earth has a frequency, and so do we, but if you're not connected, you lose that peace of mind that you find when you are in the same frequency.

I know this sounds very 'new age,' but I'm telling you this from a scientific perspective. You can match the frequency of the Earth if you connect yourself with it. Wearing comfy shoes and walking only on floors and sidewalks separates you from the Earth and its natural frequency. If you're walking on the beach, you can dig your feet in a little more.

The more noise in your life you can eliminate, the better it is for your mind. If you have kids, keep it quiet when they are studying. No interruptions. Have them stay calm as much as possible—except, of course, when playing. Play loud, with lots of energy.

Noise/Sight Pollution

Even noise from a freeway or airport can be distracting to the point of lowered IQ. Gary Evans of Cornell University, New York, and colleagues studied elementary school children's IQ as Munich, Germany, closed down its international airport and opened a new one in a neighboring city. The reading, long-term memory, and speech scores of the children dropped significantly as the new airport opened, and the test scores rose substantially of the children near the old airport as the noise levels ceased with its closing.

Close your eyes whenever you can. The simple act of seeing uses 30–50 percent of your brainpower. If you're a passenger in a car, close your eyes. Close your eyes when you're sitting on the couch. Your brain will assume you are getting ready to sleep, and it will calm down, allowing you to relax more efficiently or concentrate on something meaningful. This makes it much harder to watch TV, but if you did, you'd find you are more relaxed, and you'll have an excellent idea of what's going on just by listening. I am half-joking. It's vastly better not to watch tv at all. It quiets your mind slightly, but you are still very engaged and absorbing all of the data—the storyline, every word spoken and its meanings, not to mention the light from the tv screen and the sounds, and on and on. Merely sitting in a quiet space for 5 minutes with your eyes closed and no distractions will slow your brain and heart rate down. Your entire system gets a break.

One of the single biggest drains on the mental capacity that has ever existed is the TV—the internet and cat videos are catching up exponentially.

You have a little more control over eliminating distractions at home, but you might not have as much control at work. Please do what you can. Merely being aware of distractions and being willing to handle each issue as it comes up will help. When your coworkers start to see how much more at peace you are, they'll join in and ask the same of everyone else. It's like the famous line from the movie *When Harry Met Sally*. "I'll have what she's having." Everyone wants peace in their lives. It's contagious and desirable.

I'm honestly surprised we get anything done at all, considering how our workplaces are set up. I have a feeling just about everyone's work environment is like this, unless you have an office where you can close the door if you need to. It is estimated that it takes about twelve minutes to re-engage the mind after a five-second distraction. That means if you're distracted every ten minutes, you're never fully engaged.

Those are external distractions, but the most pervasive and destructive are internal distractions. Your mental engine has to deal with your talking mind all the time unless you can train your talking mind to shut up while you're working full bore.

Drama-Free

This is a huge issue and may be so ingrained in you that you don't realize you're doing it. Please take a look at the conflict that you spend your time thinking about. The vast majority of problems we face aren't problems at all but rather form because we are addicted to the emotions they conjure up. You are in a rush to get to work because your boss gave you a dirty look before you left on Friday, and you *know* it's because you did a lousy job on your last report. It's more likely a story you made up in your head to keep yourself occupied. Whenever a story starts forming in your head and you go down that road, make sure you fact-check every statement that you come up with. As per the above, find a quiet place, sit down, reduce distractions, close your eyes, and check yourself. Did your boss give you a dirty look, or was she introverting over some problem she is facing? Was your report in top shape? How can you verify these things? Is it worth the time to find out? Am I making this stuff up? Is this worth the mental energy it'll take to solve? It's so easy to create a road that burns mental energy. There are no roads in your brain except the mental pathways you create with the same thought patterns. It's potentially a vast open space.

Imagine trying to get somewhere in your car if there are no roads and you had no feedback as to where you are. How many different paths would you take? Clearing up your mind gives you space to adapt to new situations. You can't make a turn if there's no room to maneuver. Keep your mind quiet. You'll have more mental space, and the little things won't bite you, and you'll see the larger issues before they happen. Your intuition will protect you.

For ease of conversation, let's say you have 100 mental energy units when you wake up in the morning, and as the day wears on, you use them up. The more you are introverted, and your mind is spinning over some unsolvable problem, the faster you use them up. When you don't have many left, there's not much left over to change gears or adapt to new situations.

You spill your coffee on the way out the door, it gets all over your white shirt, and you're already running late. You can feel the emotions pouring forth, and your blood pressure shoots up. You're angry now. You throw your coffee mug against the wall, shattering it. It hits the dog, who panics and runs under your feet, tripping you. You fall to the floor in extreme pain and kick the kitchen cupboard to vent your frustration—and break your toe. *Ugh!*

If your mind is freed up all the time, you have more mental energy to adapt to small issues, and you have more capacity for your intuition to tell you when something more impactful is about to happen. You won't accidentally spill your coffee when you're on your way out the door because you are more alert, and your balance and agility are at their highest.

The larger issues you'll bypass altogether. Bad things won't happen to you. Your intuition will save you—some things you will notice. You'll have an odd feeling in your stomach when a mugger is stalking you. Other stuff you'll never be aware of. You left for work 2 minutes later than usual, and it saved you from being in a car accident. Yes, your ability to perceive that caliber of event is magnificent.

If your mind is always spinning, you'll be prone to accidents and bad luck. Thinking, evaluating, thinking, evaluating. Brrrrrrrr, vrrr-rmmmmm. The engine revs. Meditation is the easiest way to learn to quiet your mind. You should go through your entire day in a meditative state unless you are actively solving a problem.

Remember the story earlier in the book about assuming Joe took your favorite pen? Suppose you are operating daily using 98% of your mental energy and something very minor like that pops up. In that case, your mind gets overburdened, and you resort to emotion to resolve it—anger. To further save energy, you jump to the first conclusion that comes to mind. *'Joe looked at your pen, and he must have liked it and taken it.'* You feel some relief because you *solved* your problem, but you're still pissed. You erroneously assume the relief you feel is from arriving at the correct solution. However, it's that you came to *a conclusion* and your mind very much wants to get this over with because you have very little energy left, and anger takes a lot of it.

If you operated daily using only 5% of your mental energy, the alteration of the future you had planned for by grabbing your pen and realizing that it is missing would only drive your usage up to 7%, and you're not in any danger of overloading. If you were only using 5%, you would have enough mental capacity to know that your pen had fallen behind your desk, and you would remember hearing it, and made a mental note that it is there, and to crawl under your desk to get it when you had time. Or even better, you would have known that if you set the pen down on that part of your desk, later when you pick up your phone, it would probably push it off, so you put your pen back on the computer where you always keep it anyway.

When your mind is overloaded, you miss many things—including where your pen went.

MEDITATE

Close your eyes and find a quiet place.

This has many benefits. Mainly, you're quieting the mind. It's not so noisy. It's taking your foot off the gas pedal—you don't need to be meditating to achieve this state. Just stop talking to yourself unless you are trying to solve a specific problem. There is an enormous amount of noise in our busy lives; white noise, noise pollution, visual noise. Just watching a busy street takes a lot of brainpower. Yes, you seem fine, but that larger part of your mind is processing everything—it's giving you a summary of what is out there, and it's doing a tremendous amount of work, and there is a lot to do. Make it easier for yourself and give it less to process.

Simply finding a quiet place is very beneficial. It can be in your car or with noise-canceling headphones. Just sit quietly, and work on not thinking anything. Music is fine, too—it'll keep your mind occupied while you don't think. I suspect that is why music is such a substantial part of our civilization; the mind loves music because it keeps you from thinking while you're listening. The downside is that it can also evoke a lot of emotion, which could suck up more energy. So, if you go this route for quiet time, I'd suggest not listening to music from your teenage years (which is usually the best kind and the most emotional). You can also whistle or hum to distract yourself. It is an easy way to get yourself to stop talking internally, but it is only the first step in getting that inner voice to quiet down.

Meditation is quieting your mind. It's merely stopping talking to yourself. Words are just a super-condensed version of what you are feeling. Consequently, putting this into words doesn't convey the full depth of what I am telling you, so please stop here and feel, in the depths of your soul, *happiness*. It's not just words. Feel the feeling.

FEEL HAPPY.

Now that you're feeling happy, practice how to quiet your mind. It can take a lot of effort at first. Your mind is doing the same thing over and over again because it likes routine. Routine has kept you alive, so your mind assumes that it is good. The mind also wants to be rewarded. Dopamine kicks in whenever your brain is stimulated with something it hasn't experienced before. It's the feel-good chemical. Simply imagining yourself making a little checkmark and getting the feeling of accomplishment is all it takes. Mentally say, "Check," and feel a sense of reward, which means you won that round. Do it when you realize your mind is drifting. Take the win! You have noticed, and you have stopped the action. Don't get upset with yourself because your mind was drifting. You do want it to stop, but you also don't want to feel anguish and pain. Always take the win. You noticed you were drifting. That is a good thing. Acknowledge it.

I suspect that overthinking will be revealed to be the cause of many of the problems society faces: depression, confusion, general malaise, aging, Alzheimer's, learning disabilities, cancer, disease, and so on. We are overstimulated by society and ourselves.

There are thirty-seven trillion cells in the human body and they have gathered together for a single purpose. They are here to survive as living organisms. Every cell is in agreement; each cell has that common purpose. As organisms evolve, it is *always* with that single purpose.

The only time invading organisms get a foothold is when our cells aren't in agreement with each other. We get thoughts like, "Am I good enough? What if I get fired? What if she doesn't like me?"—not to mention the endless bombardment of stimuli we get from marketing, advertising, the internet, tv, social pressure, opinions, likes, and dislikes. These are non-survival thoughts and utterly contradictory to billions of years of evolution. You are stopping yourself from what your cells have *gotten very, very good at doing*. Groupings of cells that are invading your body are also trying to survive. Still, you have a very distinctive and astronomically enormous advantage (or disadvantage, depending on how you use it). You have consciousness and a mind, but if you use it to turn the tides of evolution and give the invaders a chance, they'll get a foothold. On the other hand, if you keep your thoughts and feelings from spinning endlessly on problems, decisions, and opinions that have no real solution or relevance to your life, every cell in your body, all thirty-seven trillion of them, will completely and utterly dominate any invading foes. You won't get sick—ever.

Your cells are naturally in alignment; don't throw them out with needless thinking and poor thought choices. When every cell is in alignment, they work more efficiently. Different emotions use or produce different amounts of energy. Good, positive emotions use less energy overall and create their own. How much more power do you have when you're happy?

Have you ever noticed how much energy a happy person creates and uses? They stand taller, smile more, move faster. They are creating power and use it up as quickly as they make it. When you're depressed, you move slower, think slower, and put less energy into your body to stand up straight. You conserve every ounce of energy you have to keep your mind spinning. You waste energy trying to solve all those unsolvable problems that you've created for yourself until there's nothing left over for 'happy.' Using your mental energy wisely is what I'm trying to get you to master.

The simplest and fastest way to cut down on stimulation is to close your eyes. If you take the train to work, close your eyes, slow your heart rate, and relax. Use noise-canceling headphones, even at home. Your home may already be quiet by usual standards, but there is still a hum. The refrigerator, the neighbor's air conditioner, the street noise, it's all being taken in. By cutting out as much stimulation as possible, you'll have more brain power for more profound thought.

The next stage is to stop creating opinions about things that don't matter.

"IN MY OPINION..."

The Stoics had a very logical system of beliefs, which they developed in the 3rd century B.C. They have a tenet that many things in life aren't worth getting embroiled in with emotions because it simply doesn't solve them. Does complaining about the rain make it rain less? Complaining is like standing in a waterfall and being upset that you are getting wet. The idea that you don't like it is merely adding to the situation and confusing the issue. You are wet, nothing more, nothing less. What I'm pushing you toward is closer to Stoicism and beyond—well, beyond.

You don't have to like vanilla or chocolate. You don't have to have a favorite football team. You don't have to like a TV show or mushrooms on your pizza. You don't have to have made up your mind about your boss. It's very liberating to not make up your mind.

I'm not suggesting you become a robot, but remember you are using energy to make up your mind about these things and maintain that opinion. It's not locked in, so you expend energy to keep your views consistent. Humans have an odd obsession with staying consistent with their beliefs. You can't tell your wife you like beer, and then say you actually prefer wine when she comes home one day with a six-pack for you. She'd smack you one. You can move this to an extreme and not even have an opinion about your wife. I know that sounds ridiculous, but what if you just loved everyone anyway?

What if the one decision you did make was that you'd treat everyone with kindness and respect? It's a blanket decision and won't put you in a situation where you miss out. How much energy do you think you'd save over a lifetime? How much energy would be left over for doing things like loving your kids, creating an extraordinary life, solving some big problems—not little issues like making a million dollars, but the big ones, like cleaning the world's oceans.

How well do you think you'd sleep at night if you didn't carry decades of unresolved issues around in your head? Do you think you'd ever get sick if you always had energy in abundance to fight off viruses and bacteria? Remember that your brain uses 20 percent of your body's power to maintain what you are doing now. That's a pretty big draw—and that's an average person on an average day. What if you are really stuck in thought loops, and someone in your office comes to work with a cold? What if your brain is eating up 30 percent of the energy you take in from food, and it's a bit overworked simply because you're overthinking about stuff that will not be resolved if you had a thousand extra years? How likely do you think it is that you catch the cold your co-worker so generously brought to work? And how likely do you think your body would be to fight off that virus if your brain was only using 5 percent of its energy to run your life? Your body would have an abundance of extra energy to do its job and fight off infection. Viruses simply don't stand a chance.

Here's how we waste our brain energy. You have a bad experience, so you come up with a solution that solves it in your infinite wisdom and spinning talking mind. You have a lousy steak dinner. The waitress was rude (your opinion), the meat was overcooked, and the wine tasted like Kool-Aid. So, you decide the next time you go out you'll be much more decisive with the waitress, you'll order fish, and you won't even go to the same restaurant. You have very cleverly eliminated all the variables of your bad evening.

The new waitress thinks you're insulting her because you talk to her like a five-year-old, so she never checks to see how your food was. The fish was raw, and you get sick—plus, they double-billed your credit card. Now you go for another round of clever decisions, and so it goes.

As you get older, you'll experience less and less that life has to offer because you attempt to eliminate the source of your 'troubles' each day. Your opinions and solutions to made-up problems drive you further and further into apathy. You're no longer willing to try new things. It didn't go like you wanted it to go the last time, so you stay home tonight. You keep setting yourself up for failure, and it eventually gets to you. You turn on the TV or watch cute cat videos. Life becomes dull and boring. What if all these decisions and opinions you are making and holding on to are aging you and slowing you down? What if your *get up and go* is all tangled up in the things you believe? What if it's the decisions you accumulate that age you, slow you down, corrupt the soul?

Stop making up your mind about things. Don't make up your mind that you like cats more than dogs. It doesn't matter. You've just solved a problem that didn't exist. The only thing you should be doing is solving problems. If you're not solving a problem, you're wasting time and mental energy. If you're not solving a problem, sit back and enjoy the life you have created. It is *yours*, after all. The more rules you have and the more things you believe, the less significant each one becomes.

The new-age self-help gurus tell you to just *"be here now."* When you stop thinking about the past, future, and even now, you are just *here.* It's so very, very simple.

The Buddha said, "Life is suffering." That's just an opinion, and merely dwelling on that belief, whether it is true or not, is keeping you from being happy. I'm asking you to be more like the Stoics. If you're in a bad spot, you only need to acknowledge the situation. It doesn't need to be labeled bad, or good, or suffering, or ecstasy. It just is. This may sound like you'll become a boring robot, but happiness is never dull.

Have you ever asked a young person what they are thinking, and they say, "Nothing"? I used to think that that was just the rote answer. The truth is that they are likely not thinking anything—what a blissful state. You can find it, too (or, should I say, *again*). There will be some fear of missing out. What cool thoughts did I miss? All you're doing is taking your foot off the gas pedal. The rest of your mind is still absorbing *everything*. Have you ever looked at your watch and then realized you didn't look to see what time it was? You're on autopilot. Your mind has gotten so used to wasting energy, and it just dumps it out there. Your mind wastes like pioneers did in early America—chop down trees, burn them for firewood, catch all the fish out there and throw the rejects in a pile. Kill everything, take what you want. We waste and kill our mental energy. If you learn to channel your energy, you'll have more. You'll be more at peace. You won't worry, and others will see and feel your good energy. Good things and good people will be attracted to you. They'll see you walking down the street. They'll smile after you pass by, and it'll make their day.

An individuals' goal in a civilization is to bring things into existence via that thin pane of glass we call the conscious mind, that thin layer of you that talks to yourself has opinions and makes up your mind to exercise tomorrow instead of today. We believe we are in this thin layer, and we create things by pulling them out of thin air into existence.

It's the difference between the physical world and what we dream and think about. Or, more scientifically, it's the space between the atoms. The solid stuff seems more real, but that's just because all our senses can take in data from it. You can only smell particles in the air. You see objects when light bounces off of them. We simply don't have very good tools to get at the vast majority of what is out there, or we don't use them enough to develop their real power—intuition, imagination, etc.

What if you were outside that thin layer and reaching in? What if you operated from the void instead of the solid place where our senses perceive things—where it sees a very, very small amount of what is out there? All the problems you have exist because you think you are a solid human being and need energy to make things. The reverse is much more effective and is where happiness and peace lay.

Instead of materializing things into that thin layer, break down that thin veil of existence and live in a much larger space. You can simply *be*, and your mind will be free to experience new adventures. You'll lose track of time, and you won't care, you won't have problems or worries, you'll be happy out here. There are no restrictions, and you are limitless.

We evolved over billions of years. It is in our deepest DNA to survive. Every cell in your body and every grouping of cells is not *trying* to survive; it merely survives. That is all. It is the reason for its own existence, yet we, as a species, have come to believe that we need to talk ourselves through it. Bah!

This may be the most important and impactful thing I have ever told you. I hope you find it useful.

Approx. 3,800,000,000 years ago, a cell divided. I don't know why, but it did. It doesn't matter if it was God's hand or a chemical reaction. It simply divided, and it hasn't stopped. One cell divided into two, those two divided again. In a mere 5 minutes, there were 100,000 cells. That was 3.8 billion years ago.

They started to gather together with a single purpose. Survive.

Now, we have 7 billion humans, 8.7 million different animal species, 390,000 different plant species, 900,000 different insect species, and on and on.

Those cells are still dividing now, this very moment, and with the same purpose. That is a very long and persistent purpose. That's a legacy like nothing you've ever imagined. It's the reason you're here. You have that purpose behind you. You couldn't stop it if you tried, and yet you do.

You were born into that legacy, yet you resist, complain, hesitate, get depressed, don't act on what you know, miss opportunities, hate, and argue.

You are on the winning team. You couldn't change that if you tried.

Every cell in your body and in the Universe wants to survive. Why do you resist? Being negative is a complete and utter waste of energy, and yet you entice others into your way of thinking. **All negativity is created in the mind.**

You lack answers, so you complain and push back against a force that wants nothing but survival and your happiness. There is more of us, and we are more powerful than you realize. We will always win. We have momentum. We have been practicing this for a very long time, and we have gotten good at it. Stop resisting; it's futile.

Create some good in the world. It's far and away easier for all of us if you do. Stop the negativity—all of it. It's easier than you think. It's actually because you 'think' in the wrong direction. Negativity sucks up all of the energy the rest of us work hard to create for you. It's an attempt to wear us out. You will never win at this game.

With the introduction of 'big data,' scientists have concluded that the world population will stop increasing and reach a balance. As countries become more affluent and educated, they tend to have fewer babies. Scientists will tell you that more impoverished societies have more kids to grow crops and keep the family unit viable. This is a little misguided. The truth is cellular. All cells want to survive, either as their own entity or by procreating. Poor societies have more kids because their individual life is more at risk. The cells can feel the body's stress, so to continue to exist, they must divide and procreate—by making babies. Even in early America, a couple might have ten kids. Nine of them were likely to die before seeing adulthood. Life was tough. A couple would have multiple children knowing most wouldn't make it. They didn't lack food. They had to work for it, but it was there. The culprit was deeper. The infant mortality rate was 12% (it's currently about 1%). Disease and bacteria were rampant—the solution, on a cellular level, was to have more kids.

The more educated and affluent a society becomes the fewer offspring they have. Scientists will tell you it's because they are busy working on their careers, etc., and refrain from having kids. The real reason is that the body knows it's going to be fine on a cellular level. They are not in danger, and they will continue to survive as they are. There will be dinner on the table this evening. There are no worries about making it as a species—and so on a cellular level, there's less desire to procreate. We are doing fine. Society is doing well enough that my kids' kids will be fine. We don't need to have ten kids so that one might carry on. This isn't a conscious decision—although the talking mind probably makes up a reason. The subconscious mind sends some creative ideas to the spinal column, like 'Life is good'. There's no danger. You don't need more offspring.

I only bring this up to point out that your cells have been evolving for a long time. They have this survival thing pretty wired. Let that part of you do what it does best.

You're going to do that without any effort at all. You feel hungry, and you go find some food. It's the complexities of our civilization and your chit-chatty mind that makes it seem like the voices in your head are helping you. Every word you say to yourself took a lot of effort to get there, yet you already knew what you were going to say. You already know the answers you seek, but your talking brain is so busy that it's not listening to the real answers. Sometimes the best answer isn't palatable. You want a great job, but your favorite TV show is on, and updating your resume seems like too much work. Society says we don't work on the weekend. How contrived is that? Your soul doesn't care what day of the week it is.

Your concept of existence is backward. You believe you are the thin layer we call the physical universe—the things we can interpret with our senses—and that you create your life and the things you want from here. You believe that you reach out from here and pull into existence the items you want. This thin layer you call reality, that you feel is your base, results from the rest of this stuff. It is secondary. If you want to see enlightenment, you need to work from the other direction. You need to be on the outside. This is where all the energy is. It is where you create from, and from here, you create the things you want in life. You solidify them into being. You are trying to be in the solid stuff, make a million dollars, and get a house on the beach. You're pushing all this material stuff around like mad, pushing, and pulling. No wonder you're frustrated and tired and need to sleep a third of your life.

An artist is on the patio of her beautiful top-floor studio apartment. The sun is beaming, and there's a slight breeze. She has all her paints and brushes at hand and is standing in front of a large, blank canvas. She pauses, takes a deep breath, and begins creating. Time stops. She's no longer thinking—she's doing. She's in action and goes all night, nonstop. The result is a masterpiece. Where did it come from? She created it. The conventional thinking would say that she was in her studio, and she pulled from the Universe whatever she needed to congeal that idea onto canvas. Conventional thinking would say that she was in that thin layer. I'm suggesting she was in a vast nothing-ness and *pushed* the art into existence. It's much easier and efficient to push from the outside in than to pretend you are *in* and pull things toward you.

Her body may have been standing in front of that canvas, but *she* was not there. Where she existed, there was no time or space. From there, she pushed that masterpiece onto the canvas.

Everything you've been taught about life has been to keep you in that thin layer. To get to the next level is to be outside and push things *into* existence, so you can have nice things—assuming you still feel the desire to have them. The vast majority of things you think you want were planted there by society. Do you really want a Lamborghini? Try driving one. The thrill will fade in a few days. It's novelty you seek.

To be above that is simple. Just operate on the outside and *be*. There's no stress out here. It's always nice. There's no conflict, no disease, no worry. If you want drama and excitement, that can be of your own making. You don't need to go into agreement with other people's drama. You create your own fun, excitement, emotions, etc. Play your own game, not someone else's.

Believing other people's opinions and decisions is what ties you to a game you don't need to play. We have become so confused in our thinking, and we hold on to opinions unnecessarily. All of that data adds up and makes it harder for you to think in the *now*. It makes it harder to *be* here now. Every mistake you've ever made is because either you had some opinion about it based on a similar past event that is no longer relevant, or you believed someone else's opinion and so had misleading data. Have you ever seen a child make a huge mess, completely thrilled about their creation? An adult then reprimands them, "Don't ever do that again—look at the mess you've made." Opinion! Now the kid is afraid to create or has a sinking feeling that experiencing true joy will get her in trouble, all based on someone else's opinion. I would hope a parent in that situation would congratulate the creation, and then, when the child was all done creating, teach her how to clean up her mess.

Every war, every argument, every upset, it all originated from someone's opinion—some rampant thought that he or she just couldn't let go. Afterward, you make another opinion and add more mental energy and more restrictions on your future and your ability to think clearly. It's like mowing your lawn with a blow torch—sure, it gets the job done, but it's not very efficient. Why do you even need your yard mowed? You decided it. After all, you want other people to like you because you are of the opinion that being liked is good.

I'll tell you a little secret: it's the conflicting opinions you hold on to that keep you from being liked. The groups that hold the same opinions will like you, and the groups that have opposing views will not like you. If you hold no opinions or simply like everyone, then everyone will like you back. People want to be around others who have the same beliefs they do. They want some security that you agree with the things they have decided. What if you didn't burden yourself with opinions? What would happen if you simply loved everyone?

"What will the neighbors think" evolved after millennia of us being social creatures. Starting in the 5th century in the Royal Courts of Europe, it became the norm to gain favor with your peers by undermining your *adversaries*. It was a way of getting closer to the King. Being treacherous to one party was only to get another to like you more. We are still like this today. Starting in the 1960s, the 'me generation' liberated the individual from the group, but only partially. Next up is liberation from yourself. We have a long way to go—and you, my friend, need to bypass this phenomenon altogether.

When the lion fails to kill the lamb, do you think the lamb holds a grudge? Do you think the lion's friends will make fun of him? This is the state of our evolved brain. We believe the lion's thinking brain says, "I hope nobody saw me try to kill that lamb," because *our* thinking brains say things like, "I had a bad day; I didn't sleep last night; my boss yelled at me because *he's* incompetent, or it rained on the way to work, and I'm under the weather." We come up with all kinds of *reasons* why. We form opinions about things to make us feel better.

Do you know what that means? It's very literal. I'm *under the weather*. We use the phrase incorrectly today. It doesn't mean that you're sick, it means the weather has got you down. It means you're depressed because it's raining or snowing, etc. How ridiculous are we as a species? Rain falling from the sky caused depression. A person decided to be depressed because water is falling from clouds. He could just as easily be pleased—why not? Because he carries around a decision, he made as a kid. He was sick, and it was raining, and his mom made him chocolate chip cookies and gave him lots of love, thereby cementing this 'very logical' decision—depression, rain, gets you love, and Mom's cookies. It's a survival mechanism.

Stop using words to think. Just be and go where you need to. To demonstrate to yourself and to others how much you talk to yourself, do it out loud. You'll get some funny looks. People assume you're insane when you speak out loud to yourself. Is there a difference in your sanity if you talk to yourself in your head versus out loud?

There is an excellent time to talk to yourself out loud. I know I'm telling you not to speak to yourself, but there are exceptions to everything. It helps to talk out loud to think through a problem more precisely because your brain is picking it up from another source—your ears. It also cuts down the likelihood of our rambling monkey mind taking over because you are more likely to stick to a logical pattern with sentence structure.

If you have a problem to solve, set a timer, and go for a walk. Walking occupies just enough of your brain power that it's less likely for you to drift off into random thoughts. Talk out loud about the problem you're trying to solve. It has two benefits. You're now listening through your ears, and that gives the information a better chance to be heard the same way you intake other audible data, as in a conversation with a peer. You listen. It's also beneficial because you're more likely to use good sentence structure and well-thought-out ideas when you're talking out loud.

If you haven't come up with a solution to your problem promptly, you are missing data. Find more info about your situation. DO NOT form more opinions. You can't wish data into existence. Ask yourself 'what is the solution'—if your mind is generally quiet, then an answer will come quickly. If it doesn't, you need to practice quieting your mind more and find the missing data. Two things are keeping answers from you: one, your mind is too busy counting basketball passes to see the gorilla, and two, you simply don't have all the data. The first is much more likely since your subconscious mind picks up just about every piece of data in a vastly wider sphere than your conscious mind does.

I heard this a while ago; I don't know how true it is, but it's a great example, nonetheless. The woman who wrote the international best-selling book, *The Secret*, Rhonda Byrne, was selling her home years after the book's excitement had receded. The book's premise is that the *secret* to getting what you want out of life is to ask the Universe for it. She asked for a high price for her home, but it didn't sell, so she lowered it again and again. Naysayers have said that *"The Secret"* doesn't work for her either because she could have just asked the price she wanted, and a buyer would appear. This isn't how it works. At the high price, that buyer would have to have it in his Universe, for lack of a better word. It's like the guy losing his keys at the beach. If someone had stolen his keys when he was nowhere near the culprit, he never would have found his keys—but he *unconsciously* witnessed himself dropping them in the ocean and then subconsciously knew the father and son were at the exact spot where he dropped them. In the case of the home, it simply could be that the house at the high price was not on the radar of the perfect buyer. In other words, the potential buyer at the high price simply didn't see (consciously or subconsciously) the advertisements for the house. We somehow think it's magic when things fall into place when our subconscious mind picks up on stuff and uses it to our advantage. But it's still our data. We still have the data. We just filtered it out because, at the time, it was not relevant. The data is not gone; it's just not currently accessible because you're busy talking to yourself about other ideas, opinions and trying to solve unsolvable problems.

Think of your universe like a hot-tub. By 'your universe' I mean the things that are knowable to you—everything in your sphere of influence. I'm not referring to what you *think* you have influence over, but instead the much larger picture. The all-encompassing part of you, the part that remembers everything that ever happened to you, knows that 423x687=290,601, not because it did the math, but because your 8th-grade math teacher did the problem on the chalkboard and you remember.

Let's say you have a problem. You need a penny, and you're looking down into the hot-tub and see nothing but bubbles. Current self-help methodology tells you that the Universe has all the solutions, and you just need to ask. Clearing your mind will help you see through the bubbles that are clouding your mind. You can turn off the bubbles that your hot-tub of life is creating in your mind, and you clearly see the penny sitting at the bottom.

I do have to stress that there might not be a penny at the bottom of the hot tub when you turn off the bubbles. Quieting your mind lets you see what is there. It DOES NOT make things appear that weren't there before. It is not the solution to every problem. It gives you a massive advantage over your current methods. If the 'penny' or answer isn't there, it merely means you need more data. We are in the information age. There is no shortage of data, but you have to find it. This mindset is what you need to work towards once you stop forming opinions. Fill that freed-up space with facts and data; read books, go to school, learn by doing. Find anything that will expand your mind, do it!!

Civilization fills its collective mind with something, anything. It's not always right or good.

When someone is complaining you will always know that their mind has been spinning in endless thought loops. Complaining is the result of only looking inward for a solution to a problem, and it rarely solves the problem. I want to differentiate between telling someone responsible that there is a problem that they need to fix and needlessly telling someone who isn't accountable for the trouble you have. If you were overcharged at the grocery store and tell the clerk about it, that's not complaining. If you tell that same clerk that your husband is mean and won't let you get a puppy—that is complaining, and no one likes to listen to it. It brings everyone's mood down and is irresponsible to do to someone.

Complaining is the mind's last-ditch effort to solve a problem internally without looking for more data externally. If you find yourself complaining or hear someone else doing it, gather more data from books, ask good questions of other people, etc. Don't complain about it. It's not good for any of us.

DECISIONS AND EMOTIONS

Where does *hate* come from? A decision preceded every emotion anyone has ever experienced.

Decisions are the only thing we have control over in our lives. You can't control the weather, you can't control what people think of you, but you can control what *you* think about *them*, and subsequently, the emotions that follow.

Once you've made enough decisions about something, the emotions of those decisions start to control you.

A decision to hate someone, which is always wrong, opens you up to look for more reasons to hate. You look for justifications to be right in your decision to hate them. You look for more and more reasons, find them or make them up, and then have more emotions and more decisions to back them up, and so goes the spiral into destruction.

Stop the hate at its source. Those little, seemingly unimportant decisions of hate are breeding more hate.

Practice letting them go. Good thoughts never need to be justified. Evil thoughts and actions always do. Red flags should pop up in your universe if you are justifying your actions and thoughts. Good thoughts are well beyond that. You'll find that your life is easier if you learn to avoid hate and negative thoughts.

Decide to love Monday morning. Decide to love those who are against you. Decide to learn from ignorance. Decide that it's okay that we are all different. Decide to love your job.

Life gets easier when you do. Simpler. Good things are drawn to you because you have opened up a door, a door that you are keeping shut with your overburdened mind. It may sound very new age, and *Love Is the Answer to All* type of thinking, but there is a much more practical reason I'm advocating it. It merely takes less mental energy. You can use the energy to find peace and get busy solving some big, life-changing problems. Not just for you, but all of humanity. It is your destiny. I hope I'm making it clear what you are truly capable of. Especially when you realize how much power you have. Currently, it's all tied up in the random noise that is going on in your head, like the bubbles in a hot tub.

That talking part of your brain has nothing more to do when it's quiet. You become less tense. The magnificent brain of yours is freed up to not only be happy but also get something important done—like conquering some dreams!

The emotions you experience from kind and loving thoughts will protect you in bad times. They will see you through.

I've given you a lot of information here. There is a lot to absorb, I know. I'm asking you to change yourself from the inside. Since you *are* you, it is more complicated. It would be easier to knit a sweater around your chest. It's hard to create a new you when you are 'you' already. I know you can do it. Going back to basics will help. Imagine you are brand new at this human stuff. Everything is new—you have no opinions; you don't know what is 'right' or 'wrong.' Just take it all in.

"WHAT'S WRONG WITH ME?"

There's not *one* thing wrong with you. There's a bunch of things wrong with you. You want to make some changes in your life. Things aren't as you want them to be. You're not happy, or you feel you've missed your calling, or you'd like to have more money, or you'd like your kids to respect you more. You think things would be great if you could just fix *that one thing*. If you feel that way, there's probably actually a bunch of things urging you in that direction—so if you think reading one self-help book is going to work, it won't. If you think eating more fruit is going to help, it won't. If you *know* that getting that new car or paying off that credit card will change things, it won't. You may feel better for a short time, but solving one problem is only going to open the door for another problem of comparable magnitude to slip right into that void you just created.

Your life is a breeding ground for the caliber of problems that you have been seeing.

Your mind can only concentrate on one thing at a time. You have concluded that the problem you are focused on is the source of *all* your problems. If you are sure that if you could just get little Billy to clean his room, you'd be happy, you are wrong.

It's what you believe, but when one thing gets fixed, another problem pops up. Something much, much larger is holding you back. I'm often asked, "What's the one book I should read?" or, "What's the one thing in that one book that will change my life?" There is no 'one thing.' If you are asking that question, you need a life overhaul. If your life were really in the state it needs to be not to have problems, you'd be at a much higher level spiritually, mentally, and physically. You are having problems for your level of life. Even if you fix that 'thing' that bugs you, another comparable problem will fill the void. Reading one book is not going to do it. You have to have the mindset to read *all the books.*

You also need to realize that even if there were *one book, and one sentence, and one word,* in that book, you would need to read the rest of the book to get what the author was talking about. And to understand that book, you would have needed to read other books, to give you something to compare it to. Life is learning.

In other words, you need to push the tide in the other direction. Moving a few drops of water will not stop the wave. Remember the iceberg. You are under the impression that the top of the iceberg is life. You can chip away a few chunks of ice, or melt them, or reposition them, but it's not going to change anything. The ratio of what you perceive to be your life and what is out there is an insurmountable number. Unless, of course, you operate on the other side, and reach your hand *in* and move things around a little. That's if you still care about the daily minutiae. I'm out here, reaching in to you. I'm happy all the time. It's nice.

Cause or Effect?

Adapting to your environment, or adapting your environment to you? That is the question you need to answer to break open the door to a happy, fulfilled life.

Does life affect you, or do you affect it? Being *mainstream* is a nice way of saying that you're coasting along. It's a balance between cause and effect. You are surviving, nothing more, nothing less. There's a balance between what happens to you and what you cause. It's survival.

You are insane to the degree that you allow your environment to change you. Insane people have things happen to them. Sane people make cause things to happen. Many psychology-based philosophies urge you to go with the flow or adapt to the situation, but change comes too fast, too often. If you're waiting around for a change to adapt to, ask the dinosaurs how that'll go. If the dinosaurs were a little more causative, they would've done something about that asteroid before it hit. Sure, it sounds silly, but would you rather wait for your boss to fire you or be so good at your job that it would be ridiculous for her to do so?

The more capable you are, the more you make your environment suit you. You live the life you have created. The less capable you are, the more you are embroiled by the confusion of life, the more you are affected by everything. You affect no one and are only a victim of life.

When a problem pops up, are you deterred and change course, or do you tackle the hell out of it and continue on your way?

*Don't be a dinosaur. Go make your life **your** life.*

THE GOAL OF SURVIVAL

O ur brains are set up to avoid pain more than we seek out pleasure. It was much more beneficial for mere survival to be more cautious of the stick that looks like a snake than to risk getting close to it even if it's next to some juicy berries. The simplicity of it is entropy. The Universe is decaying and breaking down into its original form. All the energy from the initial Big Bang is devolving back into its original state. We as lifeforms gather that energy, processes it, burn it up. Life tries to conserve as much energy as possible as it decays back into its native state.

The goal of a cell is to survive. It can only do this by consuming more energy as a short-term solution and dividing (cell splitting) as a long-term solution. It is only delaying the inevitable degradation of life. As a living being, you, at a cellular level, are simply gathering up energy from the Big Bang and using that energy to live as long as the power will last. Our urge to survive is the urge to move away from entropy.

Nothing wants to die, but it is inevitable. Everything you do is done to push you away from entropy and the degradation of energy.

Okay, I went a little deep on you. I want you to understand what you are up against and how, even on the lowest cellular level, you are putting effort into one thing—to prolong your existence. But you're on a roller coaster that will happen with or without your participation. Your cells will push you to survive, whether you are busy thinking about them or not. They will do their job. Spend your energy wisely.

Let's say you have a child; she is your offspring and is a part of you on the cellular level. She's very adept and studious. She's doing her homework. The overworked, spinning mind will sit with her and go so far as to hold her pencil in her hand and write the answers to her homework. This is what you're doing with the vast majority of your life. You're trying to control things that are either on autopilot or simply don't need to be controlled. She is perfectly capable of doing her homework on her own. This is purely an exaggerated example to make the point that you are overthinking your existence.

When your mind is concerned about what to have for dinner, what your boss thinks of you, what the President is doing, why the neighbor's dog is barking, you are trying to control the pencil in your daughter's hand. I'm asking you to step out of this pattern completely. You are putting your attention on things that just *are*, and it's occupying your innate abilities so completely and thoroughly that you are blind to your true capabilities. Please stop now.

We have been hypnotized to be good little citizens. It may not be a bad thing for the masses, but there's something special about you. Sadly, you're kept so busy with life that there's no time to break free anymore. Unless, of course, you break from tradition and think differently, and then not at all.

Be true to who you are. If you don't, you'll go down a rocky road of trouble and uncertainty. You'll find yourself in every place in life except where you belong. If those around you find you out (and they always suspect), they will be just as false with you.

If you are true to who you are, you'll find your place in life and have lifelong friends. You'll have your dream job. You'll have no fear of speaking your mind. You'll be truly confident, and others that are like you will be attracted to you. If you're fuzzy in your thinking, you'll attract other fuzzy thinkers.

You're looking for approval, but for what? Why do you need to be liked? Why would you want to be liked by people that don't share your same values? You're a wild stallion, and you're trying to get approval from the zebra. You don't even have to try to be liked by the other stallions. Just be yourself, and you're in. They'll come to you. It's effortless—no mental strategies, no thinking, no worrying.

It's a simple truth.

So, if you're funny, be funny. If you're kind, be kind. Never look for approval to be yourself. That's all that's expected of you as a human. Why waste your time making that stuff up?

I have given you an enormous amount of data to ponder, and I suspect that I have shaken up your thinking—and perhaps stopped it altogether. There are things you need to do as well. Practical things. Some of these things you need to do to break your old habits—some you'll need to make part of you. I've scattered these practical actions throughout the book. Some may seem silly, some are fun, some are critical, and some you might want to try a little now and a little later. It's up to you. I can't tell you which and to what extent. That will need to happen organically for you.

You can get to an enlightened state by doing these exercises I've outlined, but you have to own it. You can't just do them. You have to master them until they become part of you. I laid out these items on a gradient. Some are beginner steps, but you'll need them as a base to step off. Once there, many of these things you've learned will no longer be necessary. You will need to make those decisions as you move through your life.

THEME DAYS

Make a list of characteristics that you would like to define you. Here's a sample list: *Source, Productive, Clever, Grateful, Successful, Impressive, Radiant, Omnipresent, Energy, Focus, Intelligent, Present, Compassion, Creative, Insightful, Happy, Wealthy, Strong, Love, Inspire, Effective, Confident, Sexy, Peace, Knowing, Funny, Leader.*

Make your list, and each day, pick a word and make that the theme of the day. Meditate on that word before you start the day, and you'll be primed to see and live that concept throughout the day.

You'll start to see it everywhere. Your mind is looking for that characteristic. It's not thinking about it; it's living it. There's a difference. You're not creating thoughts—that takes too much energy. Just be the characteristic of the day. Be *confident* if that's the theme of the day. Saying, 'I'm confident,' is not as effective. Being confident is vastly different. Words aren't potent without intention.

As your day is progressing and you've gotten very busy with life, and you suddenly remember that today is supposed to be *peaceful*, take the win that you remembered, and feel the stress of the day fall away. Take a moment and feel how nice that is, and then broadcast that feeling into your future.

Tell other people what your theme of the day is. Or just tell them randomly, 'Have a peaceful day' if that's your theme. Remember, there shouldn't be a lot of effort in doing this. You're being that person. You're not *trying* to be that person. It should be organic. You are *priming* your larger mind to find these things for you. It already knows where they are, but you need to tell it that this is what you're looking for. Putting a lot of effort into this suggests that it's complicated, and your mind will make it difficult. It's actually super easy—effortless.

STARE AT THE WALL

Pick a word from the list of characteristics and meditate on it for twenty-five minutes every morning and evening. When I say meditate here, I am referring to a broader sense. Ponder how the concept of this characteristic affects your life. What has it done for you in the past? How have you not been this characteristic? What would your life be like today if you were this way all along? Or you could just sit quietly and meditate in the traditional methodology and just *be* that characteristic.

Depending on where you are mentally, it'll either start to take effect immediately or on a gradient with exponential results.

Write one characteristic that defines you on a piece of paper. Write it really big, preferably with a color marker. Make some little designs on it to make it interesting. Tape it to the wall at eye-level for a sitting position, pull up a chair, set a timer for twenty-five minutes, and stare at the word for that time. Your mind may drift this way and that but focus as long as you can on the concept of that word. Not just the word, but the feeling and idea of it. Not the ink on paper, but what the word really means. Do it with feeling. This will be the theme of the day for you, too.

There are many types of mediation. The concept has been around for millennia, and many have created their own versions. Use whatever method you like. You can simply sit in silence while looking at the word you've drawn in front of you. You can dig through your past and find memories where you exemplified the concept and explore how good it made you feel. It's also very therapeutic to look for times that you didn't exude that characteristic. Look at how different your life would be today if you were that characteristic all along. Broadcast that idea into your future. How would next year look for you if you were more *creative* all along? Doing this will prime your future. You'll look for these attributes in yourself and start to become them more and more.

You can even *preview* your day with the word. You'll do this in the evening, too, before you go to bed.

Here's the rundown. In the morning, pick your theme of the day. Meditate on that word for 25 minutes. Then preview your day being that characteristic. You'll scan through, in your minds-eye, how your day will play out, with you being that characteristic.

At day's end, you'll review your day, focusing on times and instances where you were that characteristic, then preview your future being that person. It'll start to become you!

This is one of the most useful things you can do. Make this a habit. Each day will have a theme, and you'll start and end each day by meditating on the word of the day. It's effortless and very impactful. *Remember*: the word itself isn't important, but the feeling or emotion of it is. Get the concept of the word, and not the letters that make up the word. *Strong* has a feeling, a meaning. *Feel strong!* The next day, take the next word on your list. When you are done with the list, change the order and start over.

CHANGING A
CIVILIZATION

What does it take to change the mind of a society? Is it possible?

To solve any problem, you must first reduce the variables to their lowest common denominator. Mathematicians know this instinctively, and kids are great at this when asking their parents how things work.

"Mommy, where do babies come from?"
"A baby comes from a mommy's tummy."
"How did it get there?"

You get the idea.

A philosopher has a more formidable task.

"Why is society decaying?"
"Because people stopped caring about one another?"
"Why did they stop caring about one another?"
"Because they started caring only about themselves?"

"Why did they do that?"

"It got harder and harder to make a reasonable living for himself and his family, and the stress made him concerned only for himself."

"Why is he only concerned for himself?"

"Because the most basic need for any living creature is to survive."

"Why does he not feel he is surviving?

"Others take from him or keep him from having, making it harder and harder to earn a living. Governments and corporations make it harder and harder, and poverty becomes the norm. When people are forced to face big issues and make tough decisions to survive, laws mean nothing and are broken. People lie, cheat, steal, and justify, making themselves feel like they are right. This spirals into a broken society."

This is a philosopher's tool for getting at the common denominator or real *source* behind why things are the way they are.

Sometimes I wonder where we have gone wrong— and where we have gone right, and this is the method that can be used to help find some answers.

Looking at where we are, it seems foolish to think we can change our society, but you have what it takes to change all of it. I'm giving you the tools in hopes that the fire in you becomes something... Something that others can follow—so you can lead us to a higher state. There is something quite extraordinary hidden deep inside you. You've felt it before—maybe more often when you were younger, but it has not gone away. That, my friend, is the *real you*. Let's bring it out and get it ready to make a better world.

It won't be as difficult as you might think since the Universe wants to be a certain way. There's a natural perfection in the Universe. It has a natural flow. Disturb that flow—halt it, change its path, ignore it—and you have a problem. Humankind introduced the idea of *problems*.

Before we became *civilized*, there weren't problems. Yes, bad things happened, but it was part of the natural flow of things. A lion eats the lamb; the lamb eats the grass; the remains of the lion fertilize the grass... you know, cycle of life stuff.

When we obsess about life and the prevention of bad things, we become selfish about keeping ourselves safe or getting what we 'deserve.' We end up causing more problems than we solve.

The essence of any problem is intention versus counter-intention. You want the last brownie on the plate, and your little sister wants it, too. You now have a problem, and so does your little sister, your parents, and the rest of the dinner table.

Every problem you had or currently have is your intention versus someone else's—often, that 'someone else' is imagined or is actually you. We create the vast majority of our own problems. We've become so attached to our problems; many would miss the drama of not having any and will never see peace.

If you can tap into that natural flow of the Universe, you can and will experience all the bounty you could ever imagine, and you will take those around you along for the ride. To do otherwise would cause a problem. See how that works? This is the basis of the adage, "Do unto others as you would have them do unto you."

Always consider when making any decision the repercussions it has on all life. There's more than just you.

YOUR ENERGY

Your life is in balance. All your current actions, thoughts, and behaviors are maintaining your lifestyle. It takes effort to keep that balance. If you don't believe me, don't go to work tomorrow and see what happens.

Your life has mass. It is a thing. It is a living thing. It's dynamic—it takes more effort to move or change it, but you don't have to keep up that extra effort. You just have to do something to get it moving. Once it's moving and you keep it moving, then you're golden.

You're wasting a lot of effort to keep your life where it is. First, cut out the things that are wasting energy. You can then use that new energy towards your goals.

Imagine you're sitting in a rowboat, heavy oars in the water. The fog is dense and night is entrenched. The water is choppy. Sharp little waves jab at the bottom of the boat—larger waves roll up and down.

You are rowing but can't even tell if the oars are in the water. There's no sense of space or time, nothing to help you find out where you are or even who you are—nothing to compare yourself to. It's surreal and this is what it's like in your head.

That is how most people operate. You row a little in one direction, get distracted, then row a little in the other direction. You push forward and then pull back. You lurch forward, then back, but can't tell because there is no reference point. I call it 'oar jiggle.' It's the indecisions that kill your inertia. Have you ever watched a bug crawl around on the ground that doesn't seem to have a purpose? They go one direction a few inches, stop, turn left, and go an inch more, and then make a large arc to the right and stop, and spin around, take flight and buzz around in a random path, land almost exactly where they were and do more left and right turns. I bet if you watched yourself from above, it would look about the same. This is the current state of humanity.

Over time, you'll learn to lift your oars out of the water, push them away, drop them in the water, and pull. You will keep up the pace and be moving faster than the turbulence of life. Problems will fall away behind you more quickly than they can be created. You'll look forward more often than you look behind.

If you're in a boat and are rowing, you are grabbing the water in front of you and simply pushing it behind you. You are pushing the Earth (water) out from under you and letting go of it behind you. Here's a fun way to look at it: Walk to the front of a boat with a big bucket. Dip that bucket into the water, let it fill up completely, then pick it up, walk to the back of the boat (please be careful, the deck is slippery), and dump the water over the back of the boat. Now walk to the front of the boat with your empty bucket and repeat. The boat will move forward, yet all you're doing is carrying water from the boat's front to the back. Simple. This is how you should move through life. In my little example, it would seem ridiculous to grab a bucket of water from the front to dump over the back and then fill it up again only to pour it over the front. You wouldn't go anywhere. But when you think about the same thing over and over again in your head or have the same argument over and over with your spouse, that's what you're doing. It's not solving life problems. You are just moving stuff around. Remember, humankind evolved because we solve problems. Just moving data around in your head is not solving problems. You may feel that you are improving things, but you are really just dumping water from the back of the boat into the front of the boat, and then moving water from the front of the boat to the back: no improvement, no solutions, no movement or momentum.

When you're sick, your body burns more energy trying to heal itself. It's battling all the bad stuff in your body, so you feel weak. Your body is using all of its energy to fight off the invading virus. You feel weak because there is an energy draw away from its normal routine.

Similarly, when you burn brain energy inefficiently, you then feel tired, make bad decisions, then negative emotions pop up, which use even more energy. It's an endless cycle, and you and humanity are stuck in it.

We have been trained not to get anything done. There are so many distractions now that no one thing ever gets your full attention. I'll give you the numbers again. Studies show that we are interrupted, on average, every eleven minutes and every forty seconds if we're on the Internet. It takes twenty-five minutes to get fully engaged again. You can do the math yourself, but it doesn't look good.

The ability to focus is the missing ingredient in achieving anything you want out of life. Imagine a cube. It's one hundred miles wide by one hundred deep—about the distance from New York, NY to Philadelphia, PA—and one hundred miles high. And somewhere in that vastness is a basketball, and somewhere else in that vastness is you. You want your basketball. Your conscious mind can only handle about one hundred bits of information a second, or approximately a sight radius of .005 degrees of vision, and only in one direction. But your subconscious mind knows where the ball is—it is, after all, inside the mind. But because processing data is slow and tedious, the brain picks and chooses what it concentrates on. Whatever it can't figure out, it'll blatantly make something up—but if you ask very specifically, it'll tell you where your basketball is. You can ask it.

You already know the answers you seek. You just need to dig it out of the morass of information. Sometimes simply asking yourself, "What is the answer to..." will bring about the answer. Just relax and wait for the answer. If it doesn't come, you need to gather more information, which could mean getting more data *or* gaining more experience.

The more you move forward with a purpose, the more the future picture comes into focus. When you do this, the problems of life start falling away behind you. You are moving forward, and the past begins to become the past. Your future moves toward you faster. The more speed you pick up, the less significant your history becomes.

You can see this with the balance between your bills and work.

Your bills represent your past. If you stay home and don't go to work your bills (your past) will start to become more and more important as they start to become due.

If you go to work, you are creating more stability for your future, and because you're spending mental energy on your future, your past is not as important. The more time and effort you spend on building your future the less your past becomes relevant. Even while driving the faster you go, the less likely you'll look in the rearview mirror.

The future, or what is out in front of you needs all of your attention as you'll be there in a few moments. In life, if you spend your mental energy and time on creating a better future for yourself, your past mistakes will become less and less relevant and troublesome. Your past has some control over you without you even being aware, so the more effort you put on your future the better it'll be.

How powerful is the mind? How much of an affect does the past have on you today? Earlier, I mentioned a story of boy who almost died on an amusement park ride when he was a boy, and then as a teenager couldn't figure out why he was so afraid. This is actually a true story. The boy, now a man discovered a mental exercise that was designed to relieve the pressure of past trauma. He is asked to sit in a chair, facing a practitioner that asks him to walk through, in my mind's eye, the details of that trauma. He does so, with all the detail he can remember. He goes over and over it, each time picking up more detail. And then, WHAM! He is back in the incident in every way possible except being there. His eyes are closed, but his mind is entirely on that Sizzler ride. The room felt like it was spinning, and he falls out of the chair exactly how he did during the ride some 20 years earlier. He's not doing it on purpose. His mind is so entrenched in that memory that it was forcing his body to reenact the past. His mind and body felt the Sizzler and the centrifugal force throwing him out of the bottom. He became terrified, and it changed his life forever. A memory that was lost to him was buried but not forgotten. It came out with ferocity twenty years later and knocked him to the floor. It wasn't so much the event that is fascinating, it's that the mind could be so powerful. It not only remembered *everything*, but it reenacted it in his body as if it were happening for the very first time. Everything you do in this present moment has some ties to the past. The vast majority of what your mind does for you is hidden.

In a psychology experiment, men were shown photos of women to rate their attractiveness. Unbeknownst to them, in some of the images, the women's eyes were dilated. Without fail, the women with dilated eyes were found to be more attractive. The men had no idea but would come up with 'stories' that justified their decision. A woman's eyes will dilate when she is sexually intrigued. Men have evolved to pick up on this very subtle hint. The bigger mind knows these things, but the thinking mind is clueless.

A woman enjoys singing but doesn't do it all the time. It's infrequent. She only recently realized why she sings when she does —the acoustics of where she is, have to be perfect. The interesting thing is that she doesn't think about it. She doesn't use words to tell herself, "I bet if I sing right here, in this corridor, that the quality of the sound will be excellent." She instinctively knows it will, and she'll sing whatever comes to mind. Her mind knows the spot she's in is acoustically interesting enough to trigger that action. She doesn't think about it. She doesn't look for these spots. When she's in it, she knows on a deep level. These things are innate in everyone, but we cover up those skills with thinking. We blind ourselves to the gorilla in the middle of the basketball game.

HOW WE GOT HERE

Many of the limitations you're embroiled in have come from our evolution as a species and civilization. You can get a glimpse of how things evolve by looking at our two-party government.

The role of the two-party political system has evolved into its current state as a natural progression. That same process can be seen in anything that develops. The determining factor in its longevity is whether or not those two forces are in balance according to its environment. The dinosaurs didn't have that balance. Sharks have it mastered.

Two driving forces are necessary and must work together, yet they are opposed. It's the Yin and Yang of life, the Masculine, and Feminine. They are not entirely opposing forces; they have the same primary purpose. It's not good versus evil.

Republicans are driven to move forward at all costs to survive, take risks, and find new ways of doing things. It's analytical and logical. Business drives our lives and should be given priority. In the military, it would be the drive to seek out and kill the enemy.

Democrats are driven to protect the body and take care of the struggling, the indigent, and the helpless. In nature, it's the drive to survive by being safe, nurturing, and kind. It's not logical but emotional. Compassion for others less fortunate is the priority, and all should be equal. In military terms, this would be the illogical but emotional decision never to leave a soldier behind; to risk the group's lives to save the one.

Think of the two-party system as being like a caterpillar. The head is Republican, driven to find new food. It pulls the body forward. It destroys as it goes but supplies food to the body. It takes risks by moving out on limbs, but it will fall on occasion. The body is Democrat. It slows the caterpillar's head in general but distributes the food equally among all those extra little legs.

It's a balance. One needs the other. You can see this phenomenon in everything that has evolved. For example, the evolution of the car has been to make it faster and more cost-effective to sell. The first cars struggled to drive fifteen miles per hour. Now one hundred miles per hour is pretty damn easy. The other side of this evolution is to keep it safe for the masses. We get seat belts, rearview mirrors, pollution controls, and airbags, which either slow the car or adversely affect its production cost.

My point is that there's a balance, and if it's practical, it's a natural balance. If that synchronicity wavers, its longevity is shortened.

I'm setting you up so you can solve the big problems in life. So far, what I've taught you will calm your mind—but you have to exercise it, too, make it stronger, faster, and more capable.

There is a curse among the great minds of the world. Einstein and others have feared this and have worked frantically to beat it. It is pretty well known in those circles that the greatest minds in history created their most significant accomplishments in their mid-twenties to mid-thirties. After that, they suppose, it's over, and you'll be relegated to being a University Professor.

It is not even remotely true. The thing that all of these great scientists ran into was mental distractions. They got married and had kids, they bought a house, furnished it, fixed the broken car, went to speaking engagements, got involved in politics, became celebrities. Their minds didn't get too old; they got distracted. You can have and do all these things, but you simply must master your mind and keep it quiet as much as possible. The most effective way to keep it quiet is to remove the clutter. We keep too many fixed ideas and rules of conduct and opinions rattling around in our heads that it's hard to see the real answers. The best solutions are the simplest.

If Einstein and other great scientists felt that they lost their brain powers after a certain age, but it was the distractions that life threw at them, what do you think happens to a child who grows up in a turbulent environment? How well do you think he'll do in school if he's worried about getting beat up at lunchtime or if there will be dinner on the table tonight? We, in our great wisdom, as a society, have concluded that lower-income families aren't as smart. How distracted would your concentration be if you have to hide in your closet because your father has been drinking? Or if the best meal you get is from the school cafeteria? We have much to learn about ourselves and the world we have created. We are quite insane as a civilization, but we think we're doing well because of our need to be right.

Imagine a young man in his first real job. The company is very fastidious about rules. It's his job to write a new policy. Every policy had to be spot-on and convey *exactly* what was expected and worded in such a way that no one could poke holes in it.

He's given the task of writing a rule that salespeople are not allowed to text while driving. It seems simple enough to write, but the policy had to cover every angle and every situation that might occur. What if the salesperson was on his lunch-hour but driving from a customer's office? What if he was at a stoplight? What if he pulls over? Does he need to turn the engine off? What if it's after hours but still on the job? He's tasked to include *all* situations and details.

He works on it for a few days and presents it to the boss. He immediately started poking holes in it—but for every question he has, the young man directs him to the paragraph that covers it. The meeting went on like this for an hour.

Finally, the boss tells the new employee he doesn't like it and to start over and make it cover everything.

The young man takes a deep breath and says, "But..." Then he stops, a bit frustrated.

He calls out loud, "Hey Carlos!" Carlos is the *one* salesperson. It's a very small company, and his office is next door to the boss's office.

"Yeah, what do you want?"

"Don't text while driving," he yells back to him. He says, "I don't. It's dangerous."

He looks back at the boss. "Problem solved."

The point is that you can spend a lifetime trying to write rules to prevent every possible unwanted scenario from happening. That's a lot of time. Doing it all in the beginning before you start is an impossible task. As with any to-do list, you'll never have an end. There is always more to do. More importantly, every new scenario is different, so the rules you've applied for a past situation will only be partially right for this situation. If you learn to clear your mind, you will have the ability to come up with *the correct solution for this situation*, AND do it much faster, and you won't have to spend a lifetime trying to come up with solutions to problems that *might happen.*

Trying to write a rule for every scenario will wind you up with a lot of rules. The more restrictions you have, the less likely you or anyone else will read and understand them. The mere enforcing of rules becomes an occupation. The more rules you have, the less significant each one becomes. Each new rule makes the totality of the rules less meaningful. If you have one penny, that penny means everything to you. If you have a million more pennies, that first penny is pretty worthless. Get it? It's the same with the opinions you've piled up over the years. Let go of them.

If you have one rule and enforce it, your life will be full of creativity. That's an impossible ideal, but you get the point I'm making. If you have a million opinions and rules about a million things, each one has a little less impact. So, simplify!

FLAWED THINKING

_____

There's a subtle flaw in your thinking.

It's a devious little mechanism that will forever keep you among the average, ordinary, and uninspired if unchecked. You fall into the trap that civilization sets up for you, the unknowing victim. It's what keeps you from expanding and growing. It keeps you stupid. It causes you to be fearful of being your true, authentic self.

Think of the mind like a vacuum. When you take hold and accept information, it becomes yours. True or false, right or wrong, you own it. The fact that you've taken it on means that it must be true because the truth is survival, and you like that idea, and you want to survive. The things you know are true; they must be. They have to be to maintain this illusion you've set up for yourself.

This is all well and good. Even if that information you're holding on to is a lie and it causes you trouble, you somehow muddle through. You're personally strong enough to make your dreams come true; however, things get a little shaky for you when that information you're holding on to is challenged. There's a controversy, but you've so thoroughly locked on to this information that it's part of you, and you feel threatened. You feel threatened when the information is threatened. But you're not being threatened, the information is. Your ability to observe the world is blocked because you are in defense mode. You look for more data to support the information that's under attack. It's humankind's insatiable need to be right. It's a dwindling spiral.

I had a friend who *knew* that anyone standing too close to him wanted to fight him. That information was thoroughly a part of him and got him in trouble every time he was in a crowd. He had no idea his information was quite insane or even that he was doing it—but he, without fail, would start a fight with anyone who touched him. It was always *'their fault'*, and he would spend the next several days accumulating more information, made up or otherwise, as to why this other person was out of line.

Everyone holds on to silly ideas that are rubbish, and they are usually so deep that we don't see them anymore. Racism and sexism are obvious ones, but there are more that are occluded. If you aren't living your most optimal life, you are holding on to ideas that simply aren't true. If you fear public speaking or asking your boss for a raise, you are sitting on ideas that are not true. Have you ever met someone that counts every penny of change when they buy something? She has a belief that everything has to be in perfect balance, and she is somehow in control of that responsibility.

You are not information, and you are not an idea, you're not a con- cept, you're not your job, you're not your title. Let go of these things. Don't associate yourself with them. You'll find it quite liberating. The blocks, the obstacles, the disagreements, the consternation about life will all fall away. There isn't anything you can't do once you let go of everything that you believe. You become smarter, more capable, more responsible, an all-around better person. You're closer to the real, authentic you. Your ability to solve problems is near instantaneous. You never create a problem for yourself or others.

'Can't' is a lie. We are raised on the word 'can't.' It's an opinion usually based on flawed and inadequate data. There is no way to prove that something can't be done. The only way to ultimately prove that something isn't possible is to try everything, and *that's* not possible.

You want to fly without the help of a mechanical device.
"It's not possible."
"Have you tried *everything?*"
"Well, no, not everything."

'Shouldn't' is a much better word than 'can't.' 'Shouldn't' is based on experience and still leaves the door open to 'can,' if you so choose.

We all have core beliefs. Some were drilled into us, and some are based on experience; some just seem like common sense.

In very traumatic situations, we pick up beliefs that may get us out of a pinch—maybe it was the right thing to do for that problem at that time, but those beliefs are very likely not going to get you out of the next big problem. You're applying yesterday's solution to today's problem.

A father beats his son for random things. There is no rhyme or reason for it. The dad *wins*, as he is successful, and the boy is in pain.

Later, as an adult, the boy is challenged by a dog, so he beats the dog as his father beat him. This was a *successful* action for his dad. The boy gains some confidence in life but still gives off an air of insecurity.

He gets a job with a very dominating boss; he feels intimidated and wants to hit him but knows he can't because social rules tell him it's unacceptable. He now has a problem. He has an urge to use the solution he *knows* will work but is troubled by it and his dominating boss. He has a problem based on his fixed idea.

We all have these fixed ideas. Maybe you feel that you don't make a very good employee and have a fixed idea about bosses. Maybe you have often felt you could do things better, and bosses tend to be offended by your motivation. It's a fixed idea that has driven you to be self-employed. That solution may have worked before, but if you were more aware of that in the past, you might have a pretty good job right now as an employee.

My point is that if you continuously have problems that won't go away, I promise that you are sitting on fixed ideas about it. It could be anything.

"I feel better when I smoke."
"Drinking makes me happy."
"If you want something done right, do it yourself."
"You can't trust anyone."
"Everyone is stupid."
"I have to take responsibility for everything."

People have fixed ideas so thoroughly entrenched in who they are; they can't tell it's merely a decision that they made in the past. It is now such a part of them that they can't see it's merely something they are holding on to.

When someone challenges your fixed ideas, you get defensive. After all, these are the 'truths' you use to solve problems. It's how you survive. If you get defensive at other people's suggestions or ideas, you should take a look at the things you believe. Yesterday's solutions won't always work today.

When I was a kid, someone called me fat. He meant it to be an insult. I was a super skinny kid, but I believed him. I knew he meant it to be hurtful. I went home, very sullen, then it hit me: "Hey, wait a minute. I'm not fat." It was only hurtful because I believed him. Words only have power if you accept them. Had I bought into his lies, I would have been in for a life of insecurity and misery. Had I taken on his ideas as my own, they would have become fixed into a self-fulfilling prophecy.

Ideas that you've taken on as your own and are holding on to tightly are not helping you. This is very apparent if bad things keep happening to you.

All problems are solvable. Let go of your fixed ideas.

I promise you if you do, and you find the correct solution, it will resolve and stay resolved.

The most pervasive and dangerous lies are the ones we tell ourselves.

You have more power than you think. You have the ability and power, right now, to elevate your life to the highest levels. You can make all your dreams come true. I promise you.

It isn't just wishful thinking. I'm not trying to get you off your ass, so you hustle only to get burned out in a few days. I'm telling you to do something that is entirely doable if you learn to focus on the power you have. You probably won't even get tired or worn out doing it. You'll have more energy, *and* you'll be moving in the direction of your goals and happiness.

Imagine a college student. He needs to take some take some elective classes for credit. He takes racquetball just for the hell of it. It's fun, and for the most part, he plays against his peers. One time he's the odd man with no one to play against, so he plays against the coach. He thinks he's pretty good, but against him, he's never run around so much in his life. He hustles from one side of the court to the next, diving and running into walls. Racquetball courts aren't very large. There's not supposed to be a lot of running, but he runs a marathon in that little room.

Finally, after a few games, he starts watching what the coach is doing. To his amazement, he hadn't moved at all, short of a few baby steps in any direction. Meanwhile the student is sweating like a pig, and the coach is smirking at the naiveté. He had power, and he was controlling every move. Sure, the kid was deciding where to go, but the coach was making him choose to go there. In the beginning, he thought he was dominating since he was moving all over the damn place, grunting and lunging at every pass of the ball. He was kicking ass if you were counting footsteps instead of points.

I'm not giving you permission to go out and dominate your fellow human beings. The idea isn't to beat an opponent, the point is to stop wasting your energy moving in directions that don't help. The coach had power, and he barely moved. I'm telling you this to elevate your life to a higher level. Do you know what's going to happen when you do? You're going to elevate everyone around you to a higher level too. You'll be the wing of the airplane, and you'll draw everyone around you up.

You've heard that your body is an engine. You put food in and you get energy out. You put bad food in and you get less power. This is true with you as a person and even more so as a spiritual being.

You've also heard that you get out of life what you put in. Or that karma is a bitch. Or what comes around, goes around. All of these truths are about flows.

The things you do daily are either inflowing or outflowing. You say hello to your neighbor (outflow), and she says hello back (inflow to you). It's a wash; it evens out. You work all day (outflow), and you get a paycheck (inflow).

You are where you are in life because of this balance. It's like the flow over the wing of an airplane. If the air flows equally over the top and bottom, there is neither a rise nor a descent. Day in and day out, things are pretty much the same. But if you change the wing's shape so that air has a greater distance to flow over the top, it creates *lift*, and the plane gets pulled upward.

The Universe abhors a vacuum. I don't mean a Dirt Devil vacuum. If you were to only outflow—work, create, and do things—the Universe would find some way to inflow back to you. When it does, if you only let what *you* want in, it will elevate you and create more in your life. Controlling what flows in gives you power and confidence, and you receive the things you want in life. That means you have to stop some things from coming in. You have to stop unwanted phone calls, stop diversions, prevent arguments, etc. Anything that is not pro-survival should be prevented or avoided. You're walking down the street and a stranger hands you a flyer. Do you take it or stop that inflow from happening?

You've created a flow going out, and it will reciprocate with a flow going in. For every action, there is an equal and opposite reaction. You can use that law to your advantage.

Let's say Joe works all day at his job. He's outflowing like mad. He makes cardboard boxes. He makes 1,000 boxes a day. He gets paid 15 dollars an hour, and after eight hours, he's earned 120 smackers. He goes home and watches TV (inflow) until he goes to bed. His inflow for that day is 120 dollars and five hours of TV. His outflow is 1,000 boxes. *All* the *inflow* will equal *all* the *outflow*. The Universe wants balance. It's what it does. It seeks this balance. I know you've never thought of life this way. The answer was right under your nose all along. Everything you *outflow* equals everything you *inflow*.

He could go to work and outflow more. Maybe he can get up to 1,500 boxes per day, but he's still only making 15 dollars an hour. And now he's exhausted, so he watches TV a little longer and drinks a few beers, and his life is no better.

He can take control of his life. Stop the inflows he doesn't want. Stop watching TV when he comes home (inflow) and start creating something (outflow). Maybe he takes up painting. He is now doing to his life what the racquetball coach was doing to the student. He's now attaining power, and there's more outflow than inflow. The Universe will find a way to inflow more into his life. Maybe he's discovered as an artist, or perhaps his boss notices he's happier and more on the ball and gives him a promotion. Regardless, he *will* inflow more.

Do you want to know how wealthy people get to be rich? They use this simple law. They stop inflows that don't align with their life—the noise, the distractions, etc., and they outflow like crazy. The Universe fills that void with more things they want. It creates power. This isn't about money. Money just represents energy. It's about controlling what comes into your life and outflowing like crazy. It creates lift, the same way an airplane wing does. It pulls the aircraft upwards.

You are powerful in life to the degree that you hold your space. Someone charges at you with a knife and you lower your center of gravity and use his energy to flip him, and he goes tumbling, and you haven't moved an inch. This is power.

Your boss reprimands you for not closing the deal, and you smile calmly and explain to him that you and the customer have devised a long-term plan that will be very lucrative for everyone in the long run. Holding your space is power.

You have power to the degree you can control energy. Outflows and inflows are energy.

Here's what I suggest to you:

1. Cut out all the inflows in your life that aren't helping Simply cutting out TV and Internet videos will quickly move you along your quest to greater things. That simple action may become one of the smartest things you ever do. You'll be much happier and start inflowing things that you find more enjoyable.

2. If you do have to inflow, outflow back a little more. If someone says hello to you, say hello back with a bit more energy and add, "What a great day it is!" You just created a vacuum in her life, so she'll turn around and do the same for someone else.

3. Outflow like crazy. Create things. Write a book, sing, or whistle. Listening to music is an inflow—so is reading. These things are fine, but you're trying to tip the scales in your favor. Outflow is always better if you want to elevate your life to a higher level. Create your dream life. I insist.

Throughout this book, I am giving you practical steps to practice and make part of your life. It'll help you. It'll help change your mindset, but you must be open to the idea of changing, and you have to understand that you are vastly more powerful than you thought. We all are. We have been groomed to be on this plane of existence that we call humanity. It works, but there are much higher planes. The things I'm giving you here are merely a step or two up. Get good at them and go from there.

LIVING IS AN ART AND A SCIENCE.

L iving life varies between science and art. Imagine two extremes. On the far left, we have *art*, and on the far right, we have *science*. The more random the results, the closer it is to art. If you ask 100 people to paint a rose, you'll get 100 different paintings of a rose. This is art. If an image of a rose is set up on a printing press, and 100 copies are made that are all precisely the same—this is science. One has a very predictable outcome, and the other is relatively random. The things we've got figured out and are now routine tend to be closer to the spectrum's science end. The more unknowns there are, the closer it is to art.

The better you're doing in life, the closer your life issues are to a science. Your rent/mortgage is the same every month. You go to the same job Monday through Friday. Those things are predictable. As you push forward into new territory, there are more unknown variables, and navigating them is more of an art.

The speed with which you convert art in your life to science is proportional to your ability to live a good and happy life. I would call that mastering life.

The speed with which you do that is proportional to your ability to take responsibility.

There's a lot of definitions for responsibility out there, none of which I think are adequate. Responsibility is the willingness or desire to do the right thing despite potential personal harm.

The more effectively you take responsibility for life problems, the quicker they convert from art to science. Looking at life objectively, without opinions, is taking responsibility. It gives you accurate information for making decisions in the future. Even making sure you remember how events truly happened, instead of how they might benefit you, is taking responsibility for yourself and those involved in those memories. If you remember your mom always being angry at you as a child, likely, you don't remember what you did to make her that way (assuming you were the cause). Keeping those memories truly objective and accurate is taking responsibility for them.

Practice remembering events as a sort of game. Try to recreate them in your head without any bias. That is a crucial distinction because we as humans have an overly righteous opinion of ourselves.

Try to get the memory exact and not make it about you, but about the event. Try to remember everything that happened from different points of view. Develop your memory for past events so that you can accurately draw on that information to be more creative in solving future problems.

It fascinates me how the mind chooses what to remember. We file away so many things that are simply not important to us anymore. It's not bad; it's just a way for the brain to store memory. The neurons that keep that memory in place have moved on to other things. It needs to push some memories out of the conscious mind because it requires that energy to keep you talking to yourself. It's busy doing nothing productive!

It's another huge benefit of keeping your mind quiet. I'm not suggesting that it's important to remember every conversation, but it should be easy to pull up data from your past if it is now relevant. If you keep your mind in good shape, it won't push away old data. You become a creative genius. I can't express this strongly enough. Your future depends on it. Your abilities increase exponentially with this one concept.

If you have a problem that you want to solve, and the answer, or a clue to the solution, is buried in a conversation you had with someone ten years ago, but your mind is not clear, you'll never be able to access that old memory.

Let's pretend you're more like a computer. When your hard drive gets full of data, you replace it with a new one. The old one gets put in a shoebox and then in the closet. You know it's in the closet, and you know the memories are from long ago. That's all. It's a vague idea. You're now working on a problem that was incredibly similar to the one you had long ago; you feel the same frustration. You remember being frustrated precisely like this, but the answer eludes you.

Now imagine you only use your hard drive when you're working on a particular problem. The hard drive only spins for thirty seconds at a time. If the issue isn't resolved, it stops spinning, and it looks for more data by default. You're only thinking for short spurts of time. Your power usage is a fraction of what it was, and your thoughts are concise and organized. This, incidentally, is why therapists recommend journaling. It organizes the thoughts in your spinning brain. It's one of the benefits of language—although language was also the cause of the problem in the first place.

Anyway, you now have more memory capacity. The old memories don't get pushed out to save energy. They are right there for easy use. As you get older, you have more and more useful data to draw from: billions and billions of data that you can easily pull up. Civilization is thousands of years old, and yet we still can't figure out the economy. Why is that? It's because, as individuals, we can't remember a conversation we had two years prior. Our brain's energy reserves are not only depleted; they are nonexistent. Thinking only to solve a problem makes you exponentially more efficient at *everything*.

As you know, exponential growth is what makes considerable changes. Now, as you read this book, you are much farther along than you realize. You are on the verge of really taking off. Stay the course.

There has been a lot of talk from gurus about being in the flow or zone. It is the epitome of the state you should be in. Some organizations have turned this into a business to show you how. Flow, or "being in the zone," simply happens when you are too busy doing other things to talk to yourself. Talking to yourself is the antithesis to *flow*.

Your brain automatically shifts energy where it's needed. It knows that talking to yourself is a massive drain on energy. The brain looks for ways to save energy, but you've got this awful habit of burning energy by deciding you need to leave for work by 6:04 a.m. That sunsets on Sundays are always prettier, and your big toe hurts when it's going to rain the next day, and your eggs need to be sunny-side up or you'll get cancer, dog sneezes are a bad omen, and you can't be happy unless you're rich, and money is the root of all evil. Yikes.

So, while you're thinking all that stuff, you'll never see peace. The thinking mind that uses language takes up a lot of excess energy.

It pushes out memories and reduces the likelihood of connections being made.

1. Calm down your environment.

2. Find stability with gratitude.

3. Think more clearly.

4. Gain the clarity and brainpower to solve some big problems. Not just your problems, but world problems—and not just for people, but for all living creatures.

ALWAYS TAKE THE WIN

You're about to leave for work, and you are five steps out of the door. Suddenly, you turn around and go back in. You didn't grab your keys. As soon as you walk in, your wife says, "What did you forget?"

How are you going to log this situation in your assessment of who you are? Did you forget, or did you remember?

Always take the win. You *remembered* your keys. You didn't forget them. This is still a lower-level way of thinking, although considerably higher than the rest of society.

Low—"*Yes, honey, I forgot my keys.*"

Medium—"*Actually, I remembered my keys. That's why I'm here,*" *or even better,* "*I just wanted to kiss you one more time before going to work,*" *and grab your keys and be on your way.*

High—*It's a nonevent. Don't make a decision here at all; it's a waste of mental energy. (You should still kiss your wife one more time.) The bigger 'you' knows where your keys are and knows when you need to* *grab them. You only initially walked out the door without them because you were busy jibber-jabbing to yourself.*

You simply don't make mistakes or have bad things happen to you when you are fully alert, and you are fully alert when your mind and your Universe are quiet. It's similar to a blind person whose hearing is exceedingly good. You wake up to everything around you when your mind is in top shape. The gains you'll experience get exponentially bigger over time. You wake up to opportunities to be the person you are. I am patiently waiting for you to realize this, and it's not just for me. You are going to make a massive difference in the world for everyone, for all of us. Do not take this lightly.

Many things will hang you up, slow you down. Lies are opinions that aren't true. The more intensely you believe in them, the more you'll slow down and even stop. Who knows, maybe even aging is a lie.

Lies are sticky. Life is good when it's flowing. There is the natural state of the Universe, of the planets, all living things, nature, water, energy, mass, and time, etc.

Even mass—your body, your home, Earth—at the atomic level is energy. It has a flow.

Emotions have their own flow or frequency. You can feel this in your everyday life. Anger is a sudden, volatile burst of energy. Boredom, apathy, and numbness have a much lower frequency—a slower flow.

If you have an electric stovetop and turn the heat up, you can see the metal turn red hot and even expand. You've increased the frequency of the metal.

My point is that everything is flowing. A lie puts a stop to the natural flow. Lies can accumulate and build to such a degree that civilization is built upon them.

When all the flows in your life are open and flowing naturally—and you're not keeping things from happening, you tend to be happy, problems get resolved quickly—you can tap into the solution to any problem because a problem is just a stuck flow.

All problems in life can be traced back to a stuck flow.

- A physical wound is a damage to soft tissue, which inhibits the natural flow of blood and other body fluids.

- An argument between people is a stopped flow of communication.

- Money problems are less inflow compared to outflow. You are spending more than you are making. The flows are reversed.

You can manipulate flows. If it's ethical, it creates the greatest good versus the damage it might cause, and it will continue to flow in the direction you intend. If it's not ethical, it may last for a short time, but it'll eventually bite you and those around you in the ass.

A lie that is perpetuated in our society is that being selfish can increase your well-being. You've lied to yourself that stealing from work is okay so thoroughly it had become a *truth* to you and you alone. You've stopped the money flow of your company, even if it's infinitesimal to you. It's not about the money or its value. You've created a lie that will slow, stop, or even reverse the company's flow and everyone it affects (including you).

It'll even keep you from being more effective. Now your attention is on covering up the lie. You're less effective because your attention is elsewhere. You're less observant and start to make mistakes. Your ability to solve problems is reduced. You become stupid and dull. You lose that *spark* you had as a child.

You've been raised with a lot of lies as a matter of control. Maybe it's necessary. I don't know. "You can't do that" is a big lie, but it's a lot easier to tell a child, "You can't," instead of explaining, "You can do that, but there will be repercussions, and here's what they are...."

Who knows, maybe you can *know* everything. Perhaps the idea of learning is a lie, and if you had never agreed to a lie in the first place, you would be so wholly part of the flow of life you would know everything.

A lot of beliefs change over time. A lot of truths change over time. There was a time not very long ago when science believed you were stuck with the intellect you were born with, and that after a certain age, a person could no longer learn more, and that IQ, for example, was fixed. And so, we get *truths* like "You can't teach an old dog new tricks."

Neuroplasticity is the brain's ability to form new connections, and it was believed not to be possible once you reached adulthood. The neurons in your brain could not be replaced or changed. Depending on how you consider truth, maybe it was true because civilization was, in fact, at that point in its evolution. It was at a point where it was getting used to finding facts and truths. All was very Newtonian physics, and that trickled down into society. You were good boys and girls, and you went to school, and the girls would curtsey, and the boys would say, "Yes, ma'am," and walk the elderly lady across the street. You were friendly, and you'd live well. You'd go to school, and when you were done, you'd stop learning. You'd get a job and keep that job until you retired and got your gold watch.

We believed in the clockwork machinery of how things worked, including that 'fact' that you were done learning once you reached a certain age. Maybe that was only so because that is what we believed at the time. The brain was rigid because we trained it to be that way. Now it's more of 'me society,' especially in the west—although the entire world is moving in that direction—and so goes the mind. We can mold and shape it the way we want.

If you were to ask a ten-year-old child in the 1700s to name an animal with four legs that hopped, they would give answers like, "My dog is an animal," or "I have two legs," or "I can hop." You ask the same question to ten-year-olds now, and they will list every animal they can—rabbits, kangaroos, frogs—and tell you about each of them in detail.

IQ, in general, has been rising at about five points every ten years. It hasn't yet occurred to anyone that it's a curvilinear graph. It only looks straight when you look at a short time. That will change, and you'll be at the forefront.

I'd like you to keep in mind that the gains are exponential. The human mind's improvements are very much like Moore's Law and computer chips on a circuit board: they double every twelve to twenty-four months. For millennia, little difference could be seen, but now with exponential increases, humankind's abilities will take leaps forward that we could never have imagined.

Remember the gorilla example? Everyone is holding themselves back simply because they get distracted. It's an intelligence killer. Learn to cut distractions out and focus intently on one particular task at a time. You can work on many, very different projects, but in each segment of time, that is *all* you are doing. The ability to focus is the single most crucial skill you have. You must master it.

Wake up and **focus.**

We walk through life with white noise in our heads. Learn to focus when you are concentrating and not at all when you aren't. You are separating **ON** from **OFF.** When you can focus more, any task will take a mere fraction of the time. Mastering the Review/Preview technique training mentioned later in the book will give you much of these skills. You should be so focused on your task that all of your mind power is engaged. Cleaning out your garage will take twenty minutes, not two days. **Only use your brain to solve problems. If you're not doing that, shut it off.**

Your ability to focus on one thing at a time is your measure of success. Much of the time-management and self-help community will tell you that multitasking is a farce—and they are correct, to a point. It depends on the unit of time you are talking about and the intensity of the task. Many will even tell you that you should only do the one thing where you are the most proficient. If you are good at selling your product, don't try to be the accountant. I'm afraid I must disagree. If you can segment your time so you are entirely focused on only the task at hand, you can do multiple jobs and be good at all of them. If you refrain from having negative opinions, you can plow through any workload. I agree you shouldn't do more than one thing simultaneously, but even that depends on how routine the tasks are. You can walk and talk pretty easily, but you'll often see a couple stop walking and turn to each other for the more challenging conversations that involve more profound concepts, ideas, or feelings.

You may believe that emotions can be used to solve problems. They can be, but only if you use them from a logical point of view. Even then, the results are often short-term. Getting angry to get your way or cajoling someone to win them over may work in the short term, but unless your logic is sound, they will sniff you out as a fraud. Sometimes it takes a little emotion to get someone's attention, but your solution better work whether that was needed or not.

Some of these things may seem hardcore to you, but it's because you have opinions about them. Those opinions lock your decisions in place. It's the cement that holds your life in place.

Let go of the mainstream ideals you've been brought up with; eat, sleep, and get things done, and have some fun.

These methods will blow open doors.

BEING SUPER EFFICIENT

I want you to confront life like a boxer approaches a match. Before the fight, he'll sit in his corner, previewing what is about to happen. He's in **deep** concentration, focusing on his strategy and what is about to unfold. He's not even thinking—he's in the moment, but the fight hasn't started yet. Time stops.

The bell rings, and he goes in. He's not thinking about his drive home or the bills he has to pay, or that his wife's birthday is tomorrow. There is *only one thing* on his mind. He executes.

When you have a task to be done, get everything you need in one spot. If you are going to tackle your emails, for example, get a glass of water, any paperwork you need, a pen and paper, turn off your phone, and turn off anything that might distract you, let your dog out, put a do not disturb sign on your office door. Go to the bathroom now, so you don't have to stop what you're doing once you start. Predetermine what might interrupt you and take care of it now. Start a timer for a set time. I like using twenty-five minutes. If you have trouble concentrating intensely for that long, start with a shorter time frame. Open your email program, take a few seconds to preview what you are about to delve into, then go!

While you're doing it, this is *all* you are doing until you are either done or the timer rings. You're not stopping once in a while to check social media. You're not getting up to get something to eat. You are all in. If your mind starts to drift, take the win that you noticed. Do not reprimand yourself for drifting, but reward yourself for noticing. Then get back to it. Your goal is to finish before the bell rings. It's like taking a test in high school. You have to get done before the bell rings. If you want to do something else, it needs to wait. If some brilliant idea pops into your head, and you don't want to forget, jot it down, and then continue what you're doing. When the bell rings, take a quick break. Get up, walk around. Then start a new timer to either continue or get onto the next task. Do this a few times in a row, then take a more extended break, go for a walk, check your social media, do something creative like sing or whistle, draw or do jumping jacks. Whatever it is, it should be spontaneous. Don't plan this part out, but set a timer here, too. You're going to forget to go back to your tasks unless you have something to remind you. It's not critical how long you set it for; it's just a reminder to get back to it. I find that five minutes is plenty. If you're ready sooner, go get 'em, Tiger.

After each time segment, or after a few, take a few moments to review in your mind's eye what and how you did. Be objective. Then go over it again, but without the flubs and mistakes and hesitations. You are training your mind to be super-efficient the next time you tackle this type of task, and any and all tasks, for that matter. Once you have reviewed as if you were at your absolute best, then preview your future as if you were going at that same *superstar* pace. I'll go over this method more later in the book. It is imperative, and I want you to run your life this way.

Mood lighting and other environmental factors

When you need to do something specific in a large chunk of time, set up that area so your mind knows what you will do while you're there. Have a spot to meditate, and only meditate there. If you don't have a lot of space, set up the situation in other ways. Turn on a dim, colored light. You can get lights that can change to any color with a smartphone app. You can set them up all over your home to make different areas in your house look much different by changing the lighting.

Sleep is vastly more important to your health and mental well-being than our society gives it credit for. It's been determined that a large percentage of car accidents are caused by sleep deprivation. A good night's sleep is imperative to a clear mind. There are many things you can do to help get a deeper sleep. Only use your bed for sleep and sex. Don't play on your computer or phone or even read in your bed. When you crawl into bed, you are there to sleep. Don't get in bed if you're not tired. If you wake up in the middle of the night and are wide awake, get out of bed and do something, and go back to bed when you are tired again.

Some products will block out all light and some sound. Try the Privacy Pop. It's a pop tent that you put your mattress in. It's strange to see in a bedroom, but it works wonders. It's like sleeping in a warm, cozy cave. It is very primal. Our brains and bodies evolved to recuperate at nighttime. Until recently, nighttime was pitch black. City lights, streetlights, the lights from your computers and electrical plugs, your neighbor's porch light all find their way into your bedroom. The more light that seeps into your bedroom, the more your brain remains a little bit awake. Give it every advantage and cut out all the light and noise. I would even go so far as to black out the windows and cover your walls with soundproofing material. During your waking hours, you'll think more clearly, wake up faster, live longer, and be sick less often.

Set up your routine with other mental cues. When you're going to study, set the lights the same way every time. You're priming your mind to get ready. Do the same thing in preparation for each specific task. If you're a writer try going for a walk before sitting down to write, then come home and set the lights the same way every time. Set up your environment differently for each task. If you are going to meditate, always take a cold shower before hand. These are just examples. The point is to keep it consistent. Next, quickly review in your head how it'll go, and then get at it. Don't mix up the routines. You are priming yourself for the given activity. If you were to take a cold shower before writing, it would confuse your routine a little. The same thing happens if you were to read in bed or watch cat videos. Your brain has been primed to sleep in a bed, but now you are watching cat videos. We are trying to optimize your time. Some routines are invaluable.

Many things inadvertently prime us. Any company with a savvy marketing department is dedicated to priming you to remember and think fondly of its products. Everything you sense is priming you for something. It's pretty well known that drugs undergo pretty rigorous testing for efficacy and safety. To check their effectiveness, they are tested against a placebo: a pill that is harmless and logically shouldn't have an effect. However, the results are typically the same from the real drug and the placebo. Scientists have found that the pill's shape and color often have as much, if not more, to do with effect as which medicine is in the tablet. Governments will allow drugs to be sold if they make a positive difference, but they don't tell you that the placebo often works just as well. Drug XYZ made the patient 20 percent healthier, which is good enough for them to allow the sale. But they don't tell you that the placebo did as well or better.

This is the power of the mind. Your mind wants to heal. You can even tell a person that they're taking the placebo pill, and they will still get better (statistically speaking, of course).

With this in mind, I took a bottle of Vitamin C pills and put a new label on it, calling it the Super Pill. I listed out all the characteristics that I use for Theme Days on the label. When I take the pill, I purposely read the label, which primes me to be the person the Character List is looking for. It gives me a nice boost—probably much more than Vitamin C does.

When a stranger smiles at you, it primes you to smile at other people. When someone notes what a beautiful day it is, you are more likely to have a beautiful day.

ROUGH DRAFT

Your life is like a story. You have ups and downs, plot twists, antagonists and protagonists. So much of our lives are random. Life events come at you, and you handle them. If you're ready for them, they are much easier to handle. Start planning out your day creatively so that your mind is primed to look for the good stuff and stay away from the bad. You can write a rough draft of how your day is going to go. Do this every day as part of your morning routine. Write a little story about how the day will play out. It should revolve around your theme of the day. Don't let this turn into a To-Do list. It's a story that you create that will include the unexpected circumstances of life, and your mind will start to look for the things you've created.

I'm being PRODUCTIVE as my theme for the day. I finish my morning routine faster than usual, and just as I'm leaving for work, I realize that if I stop at the grocery store on my way home, it'll be much easier than going later. I run into an old friend while there, and we have a friendly chat. I tell him about my projects and he gives me a referral that will help.

I feel super happy today for no apparent reason, my mind is clear, and I feel like a little kid without a worry in the world. I love the feeling of getting things done and off my plate.

I head home and the memory that I am supposed to stop at the grocery store pops in my head just as I'm at the intersection where I need to diverge from my regular route home, and I take the win that I remembered and go to the store.

I feel vigilant and unencumbered. A car swerved in front of me, and my reactions are so fast now that I give a quick little tug on my steering wheel and an accident was averted. I take the win again. While I'm driving, I'm only thinking about driving, and my mind is always clear. I'm happy.

You can be as detailed as you want. The idea is to set the tone for the day and build your immediate future so you're looking for ways that will benefit you. It's a great way of taking advantage of something that happens in your world anyway. You are always being primed for something. If you watch tv in the morning and there are advertisements for a fast-food chain, and later in the day you're hungry and happen to drive by, you'll stop for lunch at the same place. Writing a *rough draft of your day* is doing the same thing, but you're writing your own advertisement to prime yourself to see what you want to see.

MIND DUMP

It's easier to think through a problem or sort things out when you get it out of your head. There are a few ways you can do this.

- Talk out loud to yourself—it gives the data another way into your brain: your ears.

- Write it down. Writing out a to-do list, a full-blown synopsis of a problem, or projecting what your future you want gets it out of your head where you can see it.

- Draw it out. Make drawings of abstract ideas and use lines to connect concepts.

- Graphs are a fantastic way to visualize goals and targets. If you want to pay off your mortgage in 10 years, or save $5,000 for a dream vacation, or be able to do 200 push-ups, put it on a graph as you progress.

As per above, thinking is an attempt to make things more concrete, concise, and straightforward. It takes out the space between the ideas and makes it into a more cohesive concept. It is the difference between imagining a painting you are about to do and having the paint on the canvas. When you're just thinking through something in your head, it's hard to keep the thoughts in a line. That's why journaling is so effective. It forces you to see what you're thinking. When you start this process, write down every concept that comes to mind until you can't think of anything else. Once that is done, start to move those ideas along. It will help if you start to use good sentence structure and punctuation. If you're just doing a mind dump and stopping there, then it might as well stay in your head. You are trying to get those thoughts organized so it doesn't burn up so much energy with thoughts flying around inside your skull.

Talk Out Loud

As much as I'm asking you not to talk to yourself, it has many benefits. Humanity runs on it. Don't stop. Just be in control and only do it when needed to solve a problem. One of the great things about language is that it sorts out ideas and concepts. It solidifies them. It's known to be very therapeutic. It's because we are so trained to communicate in complete sentences and ideas—word structure, well-thought-out ideas, grammar, etc. It works great to calm down the busy mind, especially if you talk out loud. Sure, people will look at you funny, but talking through a problem aloud will force you to compose your ideas like you would if you were writing. There's much less spinning in your mind if you use proper sentences.

This brings up my next tip: read aloud (unless, of course, it'll disturb others). Reading out loud goes in a different *port* in your brain. You hear it audibly in addition to processing the data with that talking part of your brain. I have been doing this for years before I discovered Abraham Lincoln also did it—much to his office staff's chagrin.

Equally helpful, and for additional reasons, is to talk out loud when working through a problem, as noted earlier. It keeps your mind from rambling. You are more likely to use good sentence structure and well-thought-out sentences. You do less thinking because it is more efficient. Problems get resolved more quickly, and you are more apt to come up with an innovative solution.

WHITEBOARD

If you have an idea floating around your head, and it's causing your brain's hard drive to spin, you are much better off drawing it out. It'll stop the spinning, and you can think more clearly. The nice thing about a whiteboard is that you can erase ideas and move them around and clarify easily. It's also helpful if it's really big. There's more space for you to add additional ideas as they pop up. You can also use different colors to make things clearer. If you don't have a clear plan, just write the keywords down and start brainstorming. You can even use it to prime your mind for a solution. If you're having trouble at work with a customer, write their name big on the whiteboard and the words 'best answer' and then leave it there. Every time you see it subconsciously or otherwise, your mind will work on the problem in the background while you do other things.

GRAPHS

Creating graphs of your goals is a great way to see your progress. You can graph just about any goal as it progresses over time. You can automate many of these things with software, but something more meaningful happens if you laboriously do this by hand. The mind soaks in the real state of affairs. This is true in lots of different areas. Students who take laborious notes in class have better memory retention of what was discussed, even when their notes are taken away from them. You simply remember and understand things better if you write down what you're hearing. It soaks in. It's the same if you mull over your numbers by hand, make a graph by hand and do the calculations. You have to go deeper into thought to think your way through it. It becomes more meaningful to you, since you're more invested.

The most useful type of graph is an Accumulations Graph. Take a goal that you can convert to a number. You want a house that costs $2 million, or you want to be able to do two-hundred push-ups or save $400,000. Next, set a deadline for that goal. The next stop is to create a graph with zero on the bottom left-hand corner and your goal in the upper right-hand corner. Draw a straight line from the bottom left to the top right. This is your optimal path to your goal. Each day, or whatever time unit you choose, mark where on that line you are. If you want to do 100 push-ups in a day, 100 days from now. Your graph will have a straight diagonal line from zero in the bottom right to the top left corner of 100. On the first day, you do one push-up, and you add that data to your graph. On day two, you do two push-ups, and you add that to your graph on day two. You can draw a line and see you are on pace. If you only do 8 push ups on Day 10, you can easily see how you've fallen behind, so you know what it'll take to catch up. Don't rush this. You may be tempted to try to do twenty-five push-ups on day 3. And you can, but it's much more essential to build the habit, and doing too many at once is just going to burn you out. Regardless mark your graph each day—even if you don't do any. It becomes a visual reminder to get back on it. Your job is to keep your line as close to that standard as possible.

This linear path won't be possible for some goals, like when growing a business from scratch. It may take a while to get the groundwork up and running before you have any sales, and even then, it may take some time before things start going, but the graph will at least give you some reference. You'll always know how far off you are. Authors often use this method for writing their books. If you wanted 50,000 words in thirty days. That's about 1,700 words per day. But only hit five hundred for three days, you can quickly see how far off you are. It also serves as a reminder of how much time you have left to meet your goal. If a goal is way off, it can be easy to forget what it was and lose sight of it. Post these graphs on a wall where you can readily see them.

SLEEP

As noted earlier in the book, sleep is one of the most critical things we do. It staves off sickness and keeps us sharp and operating at our best. Waking up and going to sleep are the two most vulnerable times for the mind, and subsequently, the most valuable. You must make yourself feel *great*, *successful*, *radiant*, and every other positive adjective you can think of during these times. Start meditating on your theme the night before, so when you wake up in the morning, you know what the theme of your day will be.

Your mind is a sponge at these two times of the day. You can get things to sink in deeply. Make these times count. You simply must spend these two time frames being the person you want to be. Go to sleep, remind yourself how awesome you are, how good you are at solving problems, or how happy and prosperous you are. Feel the feeling. Don't just robotically go through the motions. Do the same with waking up. Wake up and think, "Today is going to be an awesome, kick-ass day." This is imperative.

Never go to sleep upset—though, to be honest, once you do all the things I've outlined, you'll never be upset again, anyway.

A good night's sleep, usually about 8 hours, is far and away more important than our civilization gives credit for. It is best to go to sleep when you're tired and get up when you wake up naturally. Using an alarm is simply not natural and may disturb important sleep cycles. A cycle usually lasts 90 minutes, and we move through 3 stages in that time, usually 30 minutes each. If an alarm breaks those cycles, it may take a few more cycles or even days to catch up. If you are woken up in the middle of a cycle by the neighbor's barking dog, you may never get back to sleep, but if you were wrapping up a 90-minute cycle and a neighbor's dog barking, you might barely wake up, but then go right back to sleep. The same could easily happen with your alarm.

You and your brain need this cycle to be undisturbed. Your brain's cells use this time to flush out toxins. Much like the Morning Glory flower blooms when the sun shines and closes when it falls, the cells in your brain pull away from each other during these cycles and allow used up chemicals, which have now become toxic, to be flushed out of your head.

Your cognitive abilities, such as memory, problem-solving, and muscle speed, are significantly reduced when you don't have enough sleep, or your sleep cycles are disturbed.

Treasure your sleep time. Make it a big deal because it is. If you do need an alarm to wake up, then you should go to bed earlier. Alarm clocks are not healthy.

Besides improving your mental and physical abilities, deep sleep has the most fantastic quality of quieting your mind so that the answers you are seeking to life problems have time to bubble up to the surface. In my earlier analogy of the hot-tub bubbles obscuring the penny you are looking for, I suggested that merely turning off the bubbles will reveal the answer you seek. Sleep does this to your brain. It turns off the jet streams and all that is clouding your ability to *see the penny*. Throughout history, many people have used this simple technique, namely the most prolific inventor in history, Thomas Edison.

He would ask himself the solution to a problem, and he'd take a nap. He had a cot in his office, and he'd close the door not to be disturbed, and when he awoke, he'd write down the first thing that came to mind on a notepad he kept at his side. This was his business model and the reason we know his name today.

You can do the same. Minimally, I'd like you to meditate on the characteristic for the theme of the next day. Before you go to sleep, meditate on a problem you are working on to optimize this phenomenon, and be prepared to take note when you wake up in the morning.

FOOD

As with lack of sleep, you're vulnerable to making bad decisions when you're hungry.

The two most vulnerable times for you to do something stupid, or make a bad decision, are when you are tired or hungry. Always have some food with you. Never, ever let yourself get hungry—but do not take that to mean that you should always be eating.

When I say, "don't get hungry," I don't mean you should eat a big meal every time you notice your belly talking to you. A small handful of peanuts or a few grapes is plenty. You simply want your body to use the energy in your stomach before your brain starts to get a little foggy—which you won't notice because it's *you* that's foggy.

If you're about to go off the rails and change your plan of action for the day, stop and eat a little something. Wait twenty minutes, then make your decision on whether to alter your course or not. I'm betting that you'll stay your original course, assuming it was initially made when you had food in your belly. It takes twenty minutes for your body to ask you to give it some food. Conversely, if you eat, it takes twenty minutes for it to recognize that you have eaten. If you're about to take on something like a meeting, a presentation, studying, or more importantly, about to make a decision that will impact your life, have a little something to eat first.

I can't express how important this is. Do not ever let yourself get hungry. I am not giving you a license to eat all the time or eat poorly, just don't get hungry. The brain uses 20 percent of the energy you get from the food you eat. That is a considerable amount. You need food to stay focused and operate.

You *will* start making bad decisions if you're hungry or tired. If you let yourself get too hungry, then even deciding what to eat will become a bad decision. Junk food is easy to get. The number of people who work through lunch, to save a little time and maybe finish a little earlier, are probably the same people who aren't happy and are over-whelmed by life. Keep yourself well fed and recognize when you are getting irritable that it is probably a lack of food and you're very likely to start making bad decisions.

Joe likes to skip lunch so he can finish work at 3 p.m. Usually, he'd decide to drive to his favorite beach town and have a late lunch and a beer. Yes, it sounds nice, but it was not such a good decision when he still had lots to do. Now, after realizing his past errors, if he finishes early and is hungry, he knows not to decide anything until he get something to eat. He has a light snack, waits twenty minutes for his brain to register that he's eaten, then makes his decision. He decides to go home to eat a real meal, meditate for a few minutes, and then get to work on some of my bigger life goals. It's these small, seemingly innocuous decisions that alter your life forever or keep you at a sub-par level.

If he took the other path, he would have driven thirty minutes out of his way, spent fifteen minutes looking for a place to park, then had a nice lunch and beer on the beach, yes. And he would have liked it so much that I'd have another beer, go for a walk on the beach, then drive an hour home—in rush hour. Now when he gets home he is tired from the beer and the drive, so he takes a nap, wakes up at 7:30 p.m., eats dinner, and goes to bed. The next day he's off kilter, ever so slightly. He can feel it. Joe is normally so in tune with his mental acuity that he can feel the beer from yesterday. It's minor, but he notices. He's not entirely on his game, like usual. And so that small diversion has a longer lasting impact than would first appear. All of your decisions are this way—**ALL OF THEM.**

If Joe set himself up so he's better positioned to make a good decision, the result is much different. If he eats a few peanuts and get something in his stomach, he makes the better decision of calling on an old customer he hasn't heard from in a while, which will increase his income if he can get them back. Then he goes home and eats a nice big meal and takes a nap afterward, waking up like it's a new day.

Over one day, this is not a big deal, but the actions you take now will either have a huge positive effect, zero effect or a negative effect. Keep that in mind with every single decision you make. Ask, "How will this affect my future if I keep doing it?"

This is known as the Butterfly Effect. A hurricane hits Florida, and every atom's movement is traced back to the very slight breeze a Monarch Butterfly flapping its wings in South America caused. That single flap of a butterfly's wings could have just as easily yielded a sunny day in Florida. We choose when to flap our wings, and we pick (to some degree) how today's actions will affect us in the future. There's nothing wrong with going to the beach and relaxing, but don't make it a habit. It should be a predetermined reward. I say this to prevent you from saying, on a whim, "I did good today; I deserve a break." That's an excuse, not a reward, and it's an awful habit. It's right up there with people trying to lose weight giving themselves a cupcake as a reward for losing ten pounds. It's contradictory.

EXERCISE

The benefits of regular exercise are multifaceted. It should be done first thing in the morning. It *must be a habit* and a routine. This will be the cornerstone habit that you can attach other habits to, and it's much easier than others have told you and what you have experienced.

There is a common agreement in the fitness world that you can always do one more. "One more!" is what a fitness coach will push you for. So let's start with that. We will start with *one*. Day one, do one push-up. Yep, that's it. You're done! It doesn't matter what exercise you pick but do the same exercise for the first few days at least.

The next day, do two. Done! Easy! It's vastly more important to build the habit. It's easier to do the same thing every day than every other day or every weekend. The body doesn't know it's Tuesday. It just knows you are awake.

On the third day, do three push-ups. Every day, increase by one. It doesn't matter what you do. I'm just using push-ups as an example. You could do something different every few days. The point is that it is cumulative. Day Five, do three push-ups and two sit-ups. Keep this up, and soon you'll reach a point of exercise that matches your current fitness level. From there, you can continue to increase your exercise routine to match the body you want.

Most people fail at exercise because they don't know where they are compared to where they'd like to be. How could they? If you go to the gym for the first time and do every exercise, you'll wake up the next day sorer than you have ever been. You didn't know how fit you were. You don't need to know exactly, but you do need to exceed and then keep going. You can do this by creeping up to it gradually. In the beginning all that you need to know is that you're *lower* than where you want to be. If you never exercise, your fitness level is equal to your daily activity. The idea of exercising is to push your body beyond what you do in your daily routine. If you want to be healthier, you'll need to do more than that amount, but that is the unknown. If you are a doctor that is on his feet all day doing his rounds at the hospital, then walking 5 minutes on a treadmill will not push you beyond what is normal. If you want to look like a professional athlete, you need to exercise like one, but doing that on day one will overwhelm your body, and you don't know yet what it'll take. This method sneaks up on that exact amount. Gradually work out more and more until you cross the line of your current fitness level and keep going until you are exercising at a level that will maintain the body you want. This will be the exact amount of exercise you have to do *every day* to keep the body you want. The habit of exercise is vastly more important than how much exercise you do.

What if you did this for a year. By the end, you are doing 365 things. It's a mixture of sit-ups, push-ups, arm curls, dips, etc. Then you back down to two hundred things every morning and realized you backed down too far. Your body is now a little less fit than your ideal, so you start from two hundred and added a push-up every day until you get to two hundred 'things' and fifty push-ups. Now you have the body you want, and you know the exact amount of exercise it takes to maintain it. You'll never be sore. Your mind will be ready to exercise every morning. Your day may feel a little off if you miss a day (which should be very rare). Because you are healthy and fit, you're more likely to eat healthily, and so goes the good habit stack.

LIKE-MINDED PEOPLE

Know that fear is built in. Everyone has built-in fear, and there's no reason to go at it alone. Find other like-minded people that want the same things as you do. They should be a reasonably close match to you in terms of personality, goals, and ambition, but don't look for your doppelganger. You'll likely find some people that you're not in sync with. Don't be afraid of letting go of a group or individual to find a better group. It is crucial not to maintain relationships that are harmful or hold you back. A group where all the members are aligned is much stronger than the individual.

A good coach or mentor can steer you around the pitfalls of being a homo sapiens and see things you're doing that you are blind to. This goes back to the importance of feedback; good friends or a good coach will be honest with you and tell you things you may not see.

Make sure you're getting feedback focused on progression toward an objective goal. You can use the graphs and goals, as noted earlier, but always focus on being a better you. If you're a materialistic person, know that those things will fall into place after improving the caliber of person you are, and you are likely to find that material desires fall away. We often think we want *things* to make us feel better, but it is very insignificant to feeling good on the inside.

As important as it is to find good people to surround yourself with, it's vastly more important to eliminate the people from your life who bring you down. When you get to an enlightened state, it won't matter who you are around. You will be the only person influencing you, but until then, you'll be vulnerable to the degree that you've reached enlightenment. So be wary of being affected by negative people. There are two ways of thinking; people with a fixed mindset or growth mindset. We all have a little of both, but those set in their ways are unlikely to be encouraging to you trying to improve yours. Give them a wide berth and surround yourself with others who want to grow.

A very effective way to get into the minds of the very best humanity has to offer is to read or listen to books about them or by them. In many ways it's better than having them as your friends and peers. Books are the author's most profound and most insightful thoughts. If you were casual friends with Gandhi, you still might not how he thinks. His autobiography would reveal insights that you'd never see from a friend's point of view. The self-help guru Tony Robbins charges millions of dollars to have him as your coach, but you can read all his books for about $100. You can find out what Ben Franklin did that we still remember his name. You'll understand why Napoleon was such a great leader and how other people have achieved the things you want out of life.

Since your mind absorbs everything, give it useful data, a lot of it, and don't give it access to bad or random data. Technically, it does absorb everything, but the ratio is pretty extraordinary. You take in 11 million bits of data a second, but your conscious mind filters out nearly all of it, giving you only what it thinks you want. That 11 million bits per second is whittled down to 50 per second.

FEEDBACK

There are few things more important than feedback. If you can't find outside feedback, give it to yourself. The 'checkmark' method mentioned earlier in the book is feedback that you can easily provide yourself at any time you realize that your mind is drifting. In just a couple of weeks, you can train yourself to stop yourself drifting into *Monkey Mind*. The mental energy you save might just save your life. You will be much more in tune with the world.

A group of friends are on a road trip. They're all in the car waiting for the last of their group. He runs across a street to get in with them. Everyone was yelling for him to hurry up—he's running until he sees a look of horror on one friend's face. He has no conscious idea why she looked horrified, but deep down, on a subconscious level, he knew that if he didn't stop, he was going to be very badly hurt. He feels it deep in his gut, and it only came from feeling his friend's intention and seeing the look on her face. She doesn't consciously know she is doing it. It's much too fast to have had any *thoughts* involved. He does stop and a car whizzes past. He would surely have been hit and possibly killed. If his mind had been drifting around on some other meaningless task, he would never have felt the warning of imminent danger emanating from his friend. We miss so much because we are busy thinking. Remember the gorilla example?

When you "take the win," this is giving your mind and soul feedback. It's telling yourself the direction you want to go. Even asking yourself, "How am I doing right now," and then answering yourself in a short, concise way will help clear up the noise in your head.

Do you want to know where all the most extraordinary people in history came from? They weren't born; they were made. They came from an environment that encourages very specific actions and discouraged others. Mozart was the son of a well-known composer. His entire childhood was, "No, not that way, Wolfgang. Do it this way..."

You can do that for yourself. You have already assumed that voice in your head is someone else, or at least you talk to it that way. Turn that inner 'friend' into your 'coach.'

Have you ever bought a new car, then see the same make, model, and year everywhere you go? It's because you gave your mind something to look for, you gave it some feedback, something novel, and now it looks everywhere for it. There aren't suddenly more of the car you happen to have just bought. You are simply noticing. What if you could train yourself so well that you started to see everything in your life right in front of you?

Feedback Devices

There are a lot of devices on the market that give you feedback. Fitbit, for example, is a fantastic feedback tool. Spire Stone is a similar device, but where Fitbit measures heart rate, Stone measures breathing. You can learn when your body is stressing—remember;

you are the last one to know. Shortcut that system and find out more definitively. As humans, we will naturally come up with some other ideas as to why we are stressed—or even worse, decide that we aren't stressed at all. Remember, the mind is just looking for an answer, not necessarily the correct one.

There are a lot of devices to measure your sleep, your internet time, or driving time. Everything is trackable. These devices and tricks are great. I highly recommend them, but only until you learn and understand the situation. Don't track your heart rate for the rest of your life; just track it until you know what is happening under different conditions and then move on to learning something else.

You can make up systems for giving yourself feedback. You can even give yourself points for how well you're doing and try to increase the number of points you earn every day—much like the exercise program I mentioned earlier.

POINT SYSTEM

Make a list of daily actions you want to get done. Exercise, meditate, study, learn guitar, practice foreign language, etc. Whatever you need to get done daily to achieve the long-term goals. If you want to make a million dollars, what are the daily things you need to do? If you want a log cabin on a lake, you might decide you need to save $100 a day to hit your goal in 5 years. I'm asking you to do something slightly different. What *can you do* daily or even hourly that its cumulative effect would be to reach your goal?

Break it down. The further you break it down, the easier it is to get it done. This is the same thinking as the exercise program I outlined earlier. Break it down into ridiculously easy steps. The idea is to get the habit in place first. Suppose you want to be a world-class pianist. The first day hit the middle C on the keyboard, and you're done for the day. How easy is that? For your goal of having a log cabin on a mountain lake, it's more important to do something daily that is super easy for you. Maybe you save $1 a day, instead of the $100 a day, and you increase from that super easy goal of $1 a day and add a dollar a day. One dollar a day is super easy, so is $2 and then $3. It's easy to always add one dollar. Your brain has too much to process already. Make achieving your goals as easy chewing your food or blinking.

Do that with all your goals and track how much you do each day. Each item is worth a point, or more if you must get it done. Tally the points at the end of the day and the end of the week. Your goal is to increase your points on a weekly basis. You are merely trying to beat last week's points. It's now a game. You have dropped all opinions and decisions per what I have taught you earlier in the book, so you are not stalling when you come to do these things. There's no more thinking involved here. You are no longer sitting on opinions like, "I don't like to do accounting, or I like to watch football on Sunday afternoon, or I don't like selling." You have a larger purpose, and it's larger than the opinions you have formed over the years. This is also a tool you can use with your coach. It'll give them some feedback about how you are doing. Emotions and how you feel about things are important, but your progress should be based on some facts. It's hard to fix a statement like 'I feel sad today' versus fixing a comment like, 'I am sad because my sales are down.' We can improve the sales and the emotions. Remember that a decision always comes before emotion.

To further accelerate your progress, make a list of positive actions above and beyond daily tasks. Make a list of negative things also. Assign points to each of the items—positive points for plus things and negative for others. If you stopped to have a beer on the way home when you have more important things to do or buy something you don't need and don't have extra money, points down. If you wrote an additional 100 pages for your new book, give yourself an extra 100 points.

I would also strongly suggest being heavier on the punishment side. For example, instead of having "Spending money on personal items when you still have credit card debt" equal to -100 points, you could say, "If my points are trending down for four weeks in a row, I have to send an extra $1,000 to charity."

DELIBERATE PRACTICE AND LEARNING

The old adage 'Practice Makes Perfect', is great, but practice with good and consistent feedback puts you in a flow state, and gets you closer to perfection exponentially faster. There is a big difference between *reading* and *studying*. Reading and listening to books is a fantastic way to give your mind some exercise. It is, however, a much lower gradient than studying and deliberate practice. Reading is more of a passive activity, as is listening. Studying is more engaging. It is taking the time to understand every word and concept completely. It is looking up every word you don't understand and drawing little pictures on scrap paper to visualize what you're reading. It is much more intense than merely reading, and it takes a lot more mental energy. It is asking the question, "How can I apply this to my life?" or "What makes this true?"

Deliberate practice is the same. It is the difference between going through the actions and making sure every effort is deliberately moving you toward the desired goal. If you're learning to play the piano, mere practice would have you play scales, hammering away at each key like a robot. Deliberate practice will be more cognizant of the sound and tone with the intention of making music versus playing notes. With deliberate practice, you stop every time you make a mistake and move forward from there, noting that you goofed and taking the win on your success up to that point. Its intent is not to get ten hours of practice in—its intention is perfection. It takes a lot more energy but requires a lot less time. You can make it even more efficient by using the Review/Preview or Preview/Review process, which I'll discuss in more detail later in the book.

YOUR BODY IS WATCHING YOU.

Always, always, always keep good posture and a smile on your face. You can do this for your work, for a big meeting you just had or are about to have. Your body is looking at you for cues, others do too. Have you ever walked into a party when you were depressed about something? Compare that experience to another event when you were in a great mood. You may notice this more if you're single— being around someone else can act as a buffer to the more in-depth *you* because you become like them when you're always interacting with someone.

On that note, your body has a lot more control over you than you might think. That statement would suggest that your body and *you* are two separate entities, which most civilizations have believed on and off throughout history.

If you're hungry, it can take twenty minutes before your stomach tells your brain, and you have the thought to get something to eat. You think it was *you* that decided, but your body told your brain to process those words.

As mentioned before, you'll start making bad decisions if you're not well-fed and well-rested. It's imperative. Otherwise, the cognitive power you need to decide whether to eat or not is compromised, so it can't tell you to get something good to eat. Instead, it will ask you to eat something, anything—not necessarily something good for you.

Over the millennia, different cultures have taught that the mind is separate from the body, but it is, in fact, one organism. You and your body are one. Your body looks to your brain for clues and vice versa. If you stand straight and tall and proud, your mind will assume you are winning and are ready for any challenge.

A man moves into a new home and had gotten into a regular morning routine. He would wake up, go into the bathroom, and look at himself. The mirror was kind of low, and he would instinctively lower his head to see himself. Keep in mind, he has just woken up. This is a vulnerable time for anyone. Your brains processing of data is not fully on-line so any data is taken in without interpretation. The mind sees a beaten man in the mirror, but he's only slouching because the mirror is hung too low. Standing straight and tall didn't work because the mirror's frame was at eye level, so he'd slump. That's how he started every day—slouching like a beaten man, even though it was just because of a low-hanging mirror. Then, he learned about the importance of posture and what clues the mind is looking for from the body. He raised the mirror a few inches so he didn't have to stoop to see himself. He even made sure he was always smiling when he looked at his reflection. He wanted all parts of himself to know that *He's winning at life*. Making a difference in your life is often a culmination of a lot of little things that add up.

Use every tool and device you can to boost you up. There is a tremendous amount of science to back this up. There's a great TED Talk by Harvard sociologist **Amy Cuddy** from **2012** that illustrates this fascinating subject. She talks about doing the *Wonder Woman Pose*. Standing straight, chest out, and tall, with your feet shoulder-width apart and hands on your hips. It's a triumphant pose, and your body knows it, and so do those around you. Your brain sees that you're strong and confident, and it will kick in those *I'm winning* chemicals and subvert the damaging chemicals of depression. Even something as subtle as smiling, whether you feel happy or not, will do the trick. This is where the phrase, *'fake it until you make it'* comes from, but that is a massive oversimplification.

As noted earlier in the book, the skills we have developed to read one another and ourselves evolved long before language did. You know if that stranger walking toward you is a friend or foe long before your paths meet. It's deep and psychological. We see and feel each other long before the words of opinions trickle into your head. Take advantage of this phenomenon and don't look back.

FORESIGHT

You can use a Ulysses contract here to start establishing good habits. A Ulysses contract is from the ancient fable of the sailor Ulysses, who, in anticipation of being seduced by the Sirens, had his men plug their ears with wax and bound him to the mast of the ship. The Sirens were Greek mythical creatures who seduced sailors with song and lured any passing ships to sail into the rocks to their demise. A Ulysses contract is a promise to yourself, anticipating that you'll make a poor decision sometime in the future that will bypass and prevent that bad decision from taking effect.

It can be as simple as packing a lunch when you know you'll work right through lunch if you don't. Or it can be as easy as putting your car keys on the shelf by the front door when you get home so you don't have to look for them when it's time to leave. A much more involved contract would be to promise yourself that you'll save 2 percent of your paycheck for retirement because you know yourself well enough to predict that you'd otherwise wait until it's too late. Good decisions lead to more good decisions, and bad ones lead to more bad ones, and destruction is always faster. In my earlier example, Joe was about to make the choice to go have a beer on the beach. On the surface he was thinking he'd have one, but deep down he knows that one would make him very relaxed, so he'd have another, or two. Then he'd go home and want a nap. Two hours later, he'd wake up, have dinner, and then it would be so late he'd go to bed and not get any of the other things done that needed to be done.

One of the best decisions Joe could ever make would be to build a continuous chain of habits that see him through the day. It'll give him something to hold on to when he gets hungry or tired, or wants to deviate into something that sounds good on the surface, but will have unforeseen consequences. He could simply start that by regulating his meals and start packing a lunch. He would rarely eat breakfast, work his ass off during the day and wouldn't get lunch. If he made sure he started eating breakfast, and packed lunch—it would cut out any excuse to skip lunch. It was sitting at his desk and if he didn't eat it, it would go bad. A ten-minute meal, close his eyes for ten minutes, and he's immediately making better decisions. When you're in bad habits, you don't know it because you're in *brain-fog*, and because it is *you*, you can't tell.

The unknown future is our single biggest stumbling block. If you have a plan before your day begins, you already have a pretty good idea of how things will play out. *Survive* is any organism's primary goal, and the more confident you are of your future, the less burdened you are by living. Success is being confident that your future is secure. People think in terms of money as being successful, but money is merely giving you the means to overcome any uncertainties about your future. If you're poor and have a flat tire on the way to work, you could easily lose your job. If you're wealthy and have a flat tire, you simply call for help, someone shows up a short time later, and you probably don't have a job since you don't need one. Or even more likely, you don't get a flat tire anyway; since you've always had the resources to keep your car in good shape, you get new tires long before they become worn out.

There are two factors at play here. One, your future is uncertain to a greater or lesser degree, and two, you are capable of handling what life randomly throws at you to a greater or lesser degree. Let's play a little game. Let's pretend there's two individuals at each end of this spectrum. At one extreme, a person has no idea what the future holds. He's been dropped off at the side of the road and has no idea who he is or where he is going, or any memories. He's hungry and has no idea where to get food, let alone pay for it. He doesn't have a plan, let alone any goals, he has a vague feeling of being hungry which is getting more troublesome as time passes. He starts walking along the road towards the setting sun, and then after a couple of miles decides he'll be cooler with the sun to his back, so he goes the other direction, wasting any progress he made. His life is one big unknown.

The other extreme is that he has an excellent view of what his future will be. He is at home, where every day has been pretty much the same for years. There's food in the fridge; he's wealthy in mind and finance. He can foresee what the rest of the day will bring; he knows what he'll be doing for the next several years and the rest of the day. He'll be traveling around the world. He has an itinerary, knows what time and date he needs to be at any one location, and what will happen when he gets there. If something unexpected happens, he has enough experience and resources to handle it. His taxi takes him to the wrong airport, so he makes a phone call, gets a new plane ticket, and gets to his destination the same day. He's traveled before, so he knows how it goes. It's always the same. He's staying in the same hotels; he meets the same caliber of people. Those two factors, the known future and the resources to handle the unexpected, are security.

Most of us are somewhere in the middle of those two scenarios, and the thing that trips us up the most is the unforeseen, random events AND getting over the minuscule hurdle of creating the immediate future. If you're stuck on the couch and can't seem to get up to work on a task, it's because your mind is blocked by the unknown. You haven't established for your mind what the next 20 minutes will be for you. It assumes that it is dangerous. Remember that we evolved and survived because we presume the bushes rustling is a snake and not a rabbit, i.e., dinner. It's safer to assume the future is dangerous. However, if you purposely create the future in your mind, it tips the scales in your favor. Remember the anecdote about Joe stealing your pen. If you were more alert and were always predicting the future you want, before you sat down to work on your report, you would have stood there for a moment and mocked up, in your mind's eye, what the next 20 minutes would be. You'd imagine grabbing your pen, sitting down and going into a deep concentration, writing the best report ever, giving it to your boss, and it's then used to drive the company forward, making millions of dollars for the company and securing your future.

You've mocked this up as the future that you'd like to happen, and in doing so, now that you've set your mind in motion and created a future, you'll remember hearing your pen fall behind your desk. Before you start, you just grab it and are on your way. You can map out everything in your future this way. It does two things. It gets you going since the unknown future is now known to a greater degree, and it primes your mind to the life you want. You are currently only focusing on that future, and you don't see other distractions. It's the reverse of basketball players passing the ball and the gorilla strolling through the scene. Now he's a distraction to your goal. You've laid out your future—you want to get the number of basketball passes correct and not be distracted by a guy in a gorilla suit. You don't want to be distracted by having a future where you go to grab your pen, and it's not there. This is what I mean by only using your mind to solve problems and only put it into gear when you want to solve a problem. When you are not doing a specific task, you are just there—nothing else. When you are using it to solve a problem, you are all in, and you block out everything else.

Book stores are filled with tricks and mind hacks about circumventing the tribulations of an unplanned life and how to achieve your goals. It's all useful information, but there's a gap that everyone falls into. What do you do right now? You should daisy-chain your entire day. Predetermine how the next 20 minutes will go, execute, then review how it went, then make it better in your minds-eye, then broadcast that action off into your future, then preview the next 20 minutes, then repeat. You'll link all these predetermined events together, like a chain, to reach the life you want. You're connecting each moment with feedback.

At the end of your day, do the same steps but for the day as a whole. Review how the day went, then review it as if you were a superstar, and then again even better, then broadcast your future as if you will keep doing things at that pace. You are priming your future. You are knocking away the unknowns, and your life will never be the same.

We find it easy to travel because there are roads laid out for us. There are none in your mind or your future, except those caused by daily habits. You can create those roads before you travel them. Imagine how much faster you'll go if there's a road for you. Create your future by making the road. Traditional goal setting gives you a target. That's fine, but you need a route to get there, not just checkpoints.

DREAM BIG

Dreams are free. Talking to yourself in circles is expensive.

———————————

Feel the feeling—don't talk to yourself about it. To keep from thinking in circles, write out your dreams in cohesive sentences. It'll keep your mind linear.

Thoughts are free, too. So is creativity. Let it ride.

As a side note, I want to make something clear about creativity. It's vast and endless, and you and the rest of civilization sell yourselves short. An author takes many months to write a novel, and as he is typing the very last sentence, a lightning bolt strikes his house and causes his computer to short out. His entire book is gone in an instant.

Most people would be devastated and wallow in misery, claiming that everything is gone. The only thing that is gone is little digits of information arranged in a particular order. The book still exists, and perhaps a better one. Do you think your creativity would have stopped at that moment? Creating is a verb. You do it at will. You can remake the old book or make an even better one—*and* it'll happen much faster since you just spent the last several months practicing.

People have a fantastic idea, then quickly write it down, so it doesn't go away. Why would you limit yourself so? You have an infinite supply of ideas in your head. There is *no limit*.

Dream *big*. Don't worry if your dreams seem unreasonable. Let go of inhibitions you have about what others will think of you. As a kid, I always told my friends and family about the cool things I wanted to do and be. After a while, someone said that they didn't care because I never did the things that I talked about. That hit me and stuck with me for a long time, and I don't want you to make the same mistake I almost made. We give so much credence to the *words* of others. I took a good hard look at this phenomenon. Which is worse, to dream big ideas and share your enthusiasm with those around you, but end up not executing them, or to not share your dreams or not have them at all? I get the idea of getting someone excited about your dreams and then not executing, but that just gets involved in opinions and fixed ideas of how things should be—which squishes creativity faster than being dead, and maybe it's the same thing.

So, if someone is sharing their great new idea, never squish their enthusiasm, and know that if someone squishes yours, they have their issues of not achieving their goals and being afraid to dream big. It's the dreamers of the world that drive civilization. Those that have been suppressed end up doing the work for other people's big ideas. It is essential to execute, but never stop the creative dreaming part of you. It is the dream you lead with; the *doing* happens afterward and is entirely secondary. The dream is primary and should be cherished.

All of your dreams are achievable, and there are many books and self-help gurus to help you along your way. However, they miss the very critical idea about how to get from point A to point B. How do you handle all the stuff in the middle? If you are driving from Los Angeles to New York, the path is pretty straightforward. We have roads, and speed limits, and cars, and you can drive fast. We don't have that luxury in the mind. There are no roads, except for the daily habits you've inadvertently made for yourself. This is what the Preview / Review process does for you. It puts the street out in front of you so you can speed along towards your goal. It's priming the path for you. It's using your thoughts as bricks to put a road there just before you get there. You'll need to do this for small chunks of time and large ones. Know what the next 20 minutes will be for you, as well as the next 20 months. See the entirety of the path and feel yourself traveling it with confidence and gusto.

The most effective goals you can have are centered on becoming a better person. All other purposes are secondary. There are three fundamental dynamics. Be, Do, and Have. *Be* is who you are as a human being. *Do* are the actions you take. *Have* are the things you want to possess. They need to be in that order when you're trying to get more out of life. The vast majority of us have it backward. A young boy wants to *HAVE* an expensive guitar to *DO* the cool things a rock star does and *BE* famous. It's much more likely he'll achieve his goals if he is *BEING* a musician and *DOES* the things a rock-star does, and he'll eventually *have* a rock-star life and be able to *HAVE* the expensive guitar.

Happiness and enlightenment are found in Be, not Have. Become noble, peaceful, honorable, and you'll have everything you want in life, and your desire for materialism will wane.

You move more quickly when you've moved past the unknown. Any action that is new to you is slow at first, and as you become more and more familiar with it, the faster you go. We come to know this in phrases like 'practice makes perfect,' but what you are doing is making the unknown known. Every moment in your future, from the next millisecond forward, is unknown. The greater your capacity to anticipate that future, the faster you will go. It's why you feel comfortable driving 70 mph on the freeway and not on side streets. There are more unknowns on side streets, and the highway has been cleared of distractions. It's the same with any goal you have, large or small. If you want to get out the door and on your way to work in the next 10 minutes, clear away the distractions and eliminate the unknowns by creating a future. How are the next 10 minutes going to go for you?

RESET YOUR DAY

You can take control of your life to a very marked degree. Imagine seeing your life from above. You can see every move you make. You watch yourself get up off the couch, look in the fridge—find nothing interesting, look at the clock, and go sit back down, and then do the same cycle again in 15 minutes, as if something new will be in the fridge. Much of our lives run on habits that we aren't aware of. You may comment to yourself about them, but even that is a habit. You could use your knowledge of how your mind works and build a new day for yourself. You could make a routine that uses very little mental energy, so you have more to do fun and interesting things. Remember that the average person's brain uses 20% of its energy. That is a lot. If you ate an entire pizza, almost two slices of it would go to running your brain and it only weighs 3 pounds. The remaining 7.5 slices will go towards powering the rest of your body. Your brain is a very complicated and energy hungry. This is why it resorts to habits. It's mentally less draining to stick you in a habit, good or bad.

I'm suggesting you take create habits that are in alignment with your goals and learn to use that power more efficiently. If it's currently using 20% of your overall energy, hypothetically, what if you got it down to 5%. You'd have a lot more power for fighting off infection, solving problems, or simply relaxing. Who knows, maybe you'll never get sick, maybe you'll be able to work twice as hard as your peers, and never feel fatigued.

These are the things that eat away at your mental energy:

1. Opinions

2. Negative emotions

3. Distractions

4. Being dispersed

5. Unclear immediate future

6. Monkey mind

7. Trying to solve unsolvable problems

If you are conscious of these things and stay away from them, or handle them in advance you'll be in control of your day and your life and that will have exponential results as you move through life. You'll be more in control of your emotions. They'll be room to move in and out of any emotions instead of being stuck in one.

You can purposely put the emotion of *happiness* in. When you're not talking to yourself and just being, and have cleaned away all past opinions about needless things, there is a void that forms, an emotionless void. It is just *being*. This, my friend, is enlightenment, and it is an excellent place to be, and if you feel so inclined you can come down a half or full step into *happy*. Happy is an emotion. Enlightenment is above emotion.

As noted earlier, it is crucial always to have food in your belly, but if you are trying to be productive, don't have a big meal before working. Your body uses its extra energy to digest your meal, so you'll feel tired. Instead, have a small snack, then have your meal as you're ending the second half of the day.

There are some schools of thought that say you shouldn't eat before going to bed. I have found that it is an excellent time for brain food. The body absorbs proteins and fats when you're sleeping. Since your body takes up a lot of energy after a big meal, you should give it all the energy it needs by shutting down your body and letting it do its thing.

Your mind is always looking for novelty, and walking takes a lot of mental energy. It takes a lot to keep that tall body balanced on two feet. For decades, scientists and engineers have been trying to get a robot to stay balanced on two feet. It's a struggle. We take for granted how many calculations are going on in our head and body to pull this off. While walking barefoot, the mind has an even tougher job. It has to negotiate where to plant each foot, so you remain balanced and not hurt your feet. It also connects you to the frequency of the ground. Yes, everything has a frequency, which is, in essence, what I am trying to change in you. You are out of frequency with the natural world. Worrying and mulling things over in your head has done this.

Chanting, humming, and even talking out loud realigns you, too. I have studied this practice, and I've never heard anyone look at it this way, but if you simply hum, you can feel it vibrating your entire core. Imagine every molecule of your body vibrating at that frequency, and then they'll line up all in the same direction. You can see this when a shallow pool of water is vibrating, or if you throw a pebble into a pond. It doesn't happen if the water is choppy, which is the state of most people. Their souls are like choppy water.

PUSHING SPACE

A spiritual being has limitless space but being in a body can limit the space that it occupies. She feels obliged just to take the space the body occupies.

As negative emotion starts to impinge on the being, she feels even smaller. The more and more introverted you get, the more you are in your head. When you're happy, you're outside of your head; your focus is out there, among the goings-on of life. It's a matter of how much space you can control. The happier you are, the more space you mentally occupy. The more troubled you are, the more you shrink. You physically get smaller, and your mental energy and impact on the world shrink. Most people only take up space in their forehead. Their minds are spinning so relentlessly that they get stuck in their heads.

The happier you are, the more space you take up. You can see this when a happy person walks into a room and fills the space, versus when a sad person walks into the room and people barely notice.

A fun way to exercise your ability to occupy space: Sit in a quiet room and note your surroundings. A soul uses the things in her surroundings as anchor-points. This is how you know where you are. The further out those anchor-points are, the more space you occupy.

While sitting in this room, find your anchor-points. It might be the lamp in the corner or the edge of the wall. Look around the room and establish those points.

After you get used to that, expand your anchor-points outside of the room. Use the streetlamp or the coffee shop down the street.

You don't have to see those points with your human eyes physically. You know they are there as a spiritual being, or just from memory.

Keep expanding those points of reference further and further out.

Each time you are comfortable with your new anchor-points, push them out further.

Push them until they encompass all of the United States, then Europe, then all of Earth, the solar system, the Milky Way, the entire Universe.

If you practice this enough, you will be everywhere. The corollary is if you ever feel troubled, depressed, or thinking too hard; your space gets smaller and smaller. Do this exercise to push your space, so it encompasses the Universe. You'll feel better, and you can get back to living free, happy, and effective.

THE LONGEVITY
OF DECISIONS

When making any decision, draw out a time-line in your head or on paper. Ask, "What are the repercussions of this? Not just for this moment, but what will happen if I keep doing this?"

This is true for the tiny little decisions as well as the larger, more involved ones. You decide to look at social media even though you looked just five minutes ago (your brain thinks it was five minutes, but it was twenty-five seconds ago). You need to learn to stop that action and draw out a timeline: "What will happen to my life if I keep doing this? How much better would it be if I stopped interrupting my time and focused on something more meaningful?" What if I remained focused on the task at hand and every task I started until I finished? How much more time would I have to do the things I enjoy? Imagine those benefits increasing exponentially. Maybe you'll realize you'll have more time with your kids, and because you have a tighter bond with them, they'll be less likely to get into trouble as young adults—and all because you stopped checking social media every few seconds.

Create whatever reasons you want but do it consciously and in alignment with your goals. You are doing these things anyway on a deeper subconscious level. I'm now encouraging you to take control of your future.

This exercise can lengthen the amount of time you focus on one thing. Let's say you're working away on a project, and you feel the urge to stop and check social media. You *almost* broke that chain by checking your social media— drop the decision you were about to make and take the win you recognized that would be a wrong choice and continue with what you were doing. The ability to focus on one thing without distracting yourself is a core skill. You can't achieve the great things you are destined for without this skill.

It's more important to get these little 'insignificant' decisions squared away, but the larger ones are important, too. I have a friend that needs my help, but it's a two-hour drive to get to him. If I go tomorrow, I'll be in his area anyway. When you make your imaginary timeline, you are looking at the option of dropping what you are doing to help someone. It is a noble thing, but is there a better way? This is why asking pertinent questions is imperative. It gathers real information instead of coming to erroneous conclusions in your head.

As noted earlier, we make countless decisions day in and day out. Some are innocuous, but many have long-lasting effects. 'I hate Mondays' will forever doom you to having bad Mondays. It's a wrong decision, and you need to stop that decision, but it's equally important to make the right decisions. This is much deeper than merely *being optimistic*. It's consciously setting yourself up for a winning future. Make long-term decisions that you can set and forget. Here are some examples.

"I always come with the best solution."
"I love people."
"I always find a way to solve difficult problems."
"I'm in awe of how well I anticipate potential problems."
"I like being honest and working hard."
"People appreciate my work ethic."

You should fill your life with these decisions. Please do not think of them as affirmations or mantras that you repeat to yourself. These are meant to be statements of truth that you simply believe at your core. They should be valid truths and not something that you have to convince yourself. Make them a truth the moment you utter them and move on. Maybe you did not 'love people' 5 minutes ago, but you do now! In the immortal words of Captain Kirk of Star Trek, 'make it so.'

Remember that your mind is taking in ALL the data of your environment. It can be haphazard, or you can give it what is best for *you*. You have this control over a young child you care about. All kids want ice-cream, but you can't let them have it all the time. You take control—you take responsibility, and ice cream is only on special occasions. Do the same here. Only let yourself have data from good sources—good books, uplifting music, good friends, and on and on.

Let's say there are three types of input that go into your system.

Bad, random, and good.

Bad will happen by hanging out with the wrong crowd with low ethical standards, listening to bad music, both in quality and lyrics that speak of destruction and hate, watching the news or relaying gossip.

Random is just the noise of life; the sounds of your neighbor's dog barking, ambulance sirens in the background, the tv blaring in the living-room, and the hum of the refrigerator. It's the gossip at the company lunchroom, whether you are involved are not, and mostly, it's your chit-chatty mind.

Good is self-help books and other non-fiction, meditation, the sounds of birds chirping, the wind whistling through the trees, and the positive things you tell yourself.

Let's say you have 90% random and 5% good and 5% bad data coming into your subconscious at a wild guess. Your conscious mind can only handle a tiny fraction of the data that pours in. The ratio is 11 million bits of data down to 50 bits. If you are generally a positive person, your conscious mind filters most of the bad stuff, but it is still only giving the *thinking part of you* a small fraction. If you were to eliminate the vast majority of random noise and all of the bad data, you can't help but start becoming more positive and more effective in your thinking. It gives you room to breathe and relax. Remember that bad data causes stress and sucks up more energy to maintain. This concept is what created Buddha. His name as a child was Siddhartha Gautama, the son of a king. The short story is that the king loved his son so much that he kept from him all the world's evil and suffering. The young Siddhartha was kept within the palace walls, and all the servants were instructed never to let the child see anything bad. It protected his mind, and to him, all was peace and love. He became restless and started to sneak out, beyond the reach of his protectors. What he saw shook him to his core. They were everyday occurrences to you and me. He saw a beggar on the streets, a man beating his cattle, and so on. He was seeing these things for the first time, and until then, his mind was void of the bad and random noise of life. This is how he concluded that all life is suffering. It's the data that suddenly flooded him when he was open to seeing it. Buddhism is now one of the most significant philosophies ever developed, and it came from a clear mind. You, too, have that ability, but it won't happen when your mind is overwhelmed with more data than it can handle, let alone filling it with unwanted and negative data.

You have almost complete control over the quality of the things your subconscious picks up. Cutting out the bad and random alone will do wonders for your soul.

Start to become aware of what you are picking up. Your mind absorbs everything—a noisy street, the hum of the refrigerator, the neighbor's motorcycle revving, the news on TV in the next room. The seemingly innocuous things are not necessarily bad, but it does wear away at you. You have a finite number of things you can perceive. If you also cut out the random noise of life, it will give you more space for other data that you might want in the future and for peace.

REVIEW/PREVIEW

PREVIEW/REVIEW

Stoicism was an ancient Greek philosophy that taught the benefits of not becoming emotionally embroiled in things that will be that way whether you complain about them or not. It's about fixing the problem instead of complaining about it and not bothering with the things that aren't going to change. It's about doing the right thing simply because it is the right thing. It is no longer about 'self' but 'us'.

Always do your best, and you will not have to worry about your boss giving you dirty looks. People react to what you emanate. Emanate confident success. We read each other on a profound and instantaneous level. Do not ever concern yourself with what others think of you, do what you can, as well as you can, and keep improving.

If your mind is embroiled in mulling over situations, do the following activity at least once a day—and more often when you are stressed.

This is the most potent and effective way to live. Master this technique.

I developed this technique in part from studying the Samurai. One of these days, I'll think of a better name, but for now, I call it R/P: Review/Preview. Samurai ritually imagine their death before a battle and then review the struggle in their mind's eye afterward. The idea is to foresee every move you and your foe will make. It is a rehearsal of what is to come. It's called a premortem. It's to prepare the soul for death, and then afterward, assuming the warrior is still alive, he reviews every thrust of his sword and every counter move of his opponent.

I use it for a much higher purpose: to prepare the soul for life.

The idea is to review something that has happened, good or bad. Let's just say you argued with your spouse. You'll review what happened in the past thirty minutes, do it in accurate detail. I find it best to close your eyes, but you can also write or type (which you should probably do with your eyes open). Review what was said. Be objective. Do not make yourself *right*. See it from your spouse's point of view too. Next, review your body motion, emotions, the location and time of day, what it regarded, any details.

Next, review it again, but imagine how you would have liked it to have gone. Maybe your tone was softer, or you simply communicated better. Do not merely recreate it, so you won the argument. The goal is to find the best solution for everyone involved. Imagine yourself being a bigger and better person, wise, confident, and serene. Optimally, imagine there was never an argument in the first place, and everyone remained happy and getting along. Use the same detail that you did the first time. As you are doing this, feel the emotion you would have liked—a higher feeling, like happiness, love, excitement, or grace.

The final step is to preview a future situation where a similar scenario might come up. Imagine it in great detail. Imagine yourself as an enlightened master. You are always happy and handle any problems with ease and grace. You emanate an aura of peace and love, and when others feel it, they become more at peace. The more detail, the better. Set a timer for this entire process. You should be done in twenty-five minutes. Feel good when you are done and wrap it up. Do not get too stuck doing this. You need an endpoint.

You should also do this in the other direction—P/R/R (Preview/Review/Review). It will boost your productivity like nothing you have ever seen before: Preview a situation or task, then do the job, then review how you did, then review it as if you did it perfectly.

Let's say you're going to clean the garage and you want to knock it out of the park. You want each action to be concise and accurate, like a well-choreographed performance.

Stand in your open garage and look at what you've got. Make a plan in your head. It doesn't have to be so detailed you lose track. Don't write it down. Just scan the situation and imagine yourself taking each action ahead of time. You know, if you pick up the boxes and gardening equipment in one go, it'll be too much, so see yourself moving all the small things out and into the driveway, then going back and pushing the bigger boxes to the side, so you have room to get the bikes out. Foresee, if you hang the bikes from the ceiling as your next task, the rest of the garage will open up, and it'll be a breeze.

This part is more about getting your brain primed to be efficient, not about making a plan of X, Y, Z. It's imagining a flow, a superefficient flow.

Next, set a timer for twenty-five minutes and keep in your mind what you'll get done. You don't need to hit that mark, but it's what you're shooting for.

Get to it. Keep checking your clock or make a mental note of it ticking away. When the bell rings, take a win. Feel good about what you've gotten done and feel extra good if you made your target.

Next, stand back a few feet and review what you did: the fumbles, the dropped bowling ball, hitting your head on the bikes you hung from the ceiling. Then the good stuff: you caught the broom handle with your foot as it was about to fall while you were sweeping up the dust, you spun around and grabbed a full bag of garbage just as the idea popped into your head that doing so would save you a few milliseconds in the long run.

This is training for efficiency. It is telling your mind that this is great stuff. It wants and needs feedback. You can trick your mind into thinking you did an excellent job, and if it feels that, you'll start being that person.

It may seem a bit outrageous, but it is very beneficial. You can do this for any period and as far back into your past as you like. Review the most turbulent times in your life, redo them as if they were better and better each time you go over them. When you feel satisfied, imagine what your life would be like today if you were *that* person from the past you just created. Then keep going and imagine what your future will be like as *that person.* I was not the star quarterback in high school, but my mind thinks I was. You may want to keep your memories straight when you go back to your high school reunion, but I will let you figure that out on your own. You will still know the difference, but your mind will not, and you will *be* the better person.

Scan through your high school years. All of them, good and bad. The more you do memory exercises, the better, but to be honest, it doesn't matter if the memories are accurate—as you'll see.

Scan the classes, the embarrassments, the grades, the growing pains, whatever pops up, then review it again, but as if things went better. You studied harder (or did not need to), you asked the cool girl out, you had the best friends ever, you caught the winning touchdown, you stood up straight, you didn't have acne, you weren't the little kid, your glasses made you look cool.

Do this a few times, each time making that period of time a bit better. You are doing this exercise on a timer, too, so watch your clock. It is vital to be done when you are done.

The next step is to preview the same period of your life in the future. If you choose your three high school years, you will do three years in your future, as if your past was what you just created.

If you were timid, overweight, had terrible grades, low self-esteem, and were from a bad family that argued all the time, you will make those memories a little better, and then a bit better until it is what you would have liked. Now, project what your future would be like **as if you were that superstar kid.**

Create where you would be if your life were incredible during those high school years. The decisions you made then are the basis for the decisions you are making now and in your future. We are programming you to get back on track to what you should have become if you knew how to control your destiny from the beginning.

You see this illustrated a little better in movies like *Back to the Future* and *The Butterfly Effect*, but I'm making it usable here for you.

Keep in mind you can and should do this for any length of time, for any period. It will erase the bad memories you're hung up on and create new, good ones, and you'll start being that new polished person.

The more you do the R/R/P or P/R/R, the more effective you will become. We've all gone into the kitchen and then stood there wondering why we're there. If you do this exercise before you start any new task, like getting up off the couch to get a drink, these little, tiny failures won't happen. You won't stand in your kitchen wondering why you went in there because you will have rehearsed in your head what the next few minutes of your life will be. You will not drive all the way to work and realize you forgot your computer. You simply won't make mistakes because you will have rehearsed it in your mind ahead of time. This process does two things. It makes you focused on what *you* want to happen, and it keeps your mind from drifting off into never-never land.

You can do this for every action you are about to engage in and every action you have just taken, whether on a small-time frame or a large one. Do not get too hung up on details—you are just scanning the situation and making it more efficient. It doesn't have to be perfect. You're only looking for better. Like the exercise routine, getting a little better every day is enormous. The wrong way to work out is to decide one day you need to get fit, then work out really hard and end up too sore to move the next day, so you quit. Everything should be on a gradient.

If you want to test how effective this is, the next three or four times you go to the grocery store, note how long you were in the store. Before you go in the next time, take a few moments to rehearse every move, every aisle, every reach for a product. I am betting the time will be cut by 75 percent.

You're going to have an enormous amount of extra time on your hands because you will become much more efficient. Use that spare time wisely. Your work will get done in a fraction of the time—but don't use your extra time to sit at your desk and watch cat videos. Instead, learn a new language, learn calculus, read a book that you would not usually pick up.

Rewrite your history.

I have purposely written this section last and put it at the end of the book. Statistically speaking, most people don't read the entirety of a book, any book. I hope that if you have gotten this far, you are indeed the person I am looking for, so I have saved the best stuff for last.

Your entire life, you have been taking in an incomprehensible amount of data. By the age of 40, you have had over a billion thoughts, and your larger mind is consuming 11 million bits of data **every second**. Your conscious mind filters almost all that data out and considers it unnecessary. It can only process 50 bits per second. That is almost a trillion bits of information in total by the age of 40, but we are only consciously aware of 0.0000005% of what we take in.

Every decision you have ever made lead you here, to this very moment. Some decisions were major, like deciding to quit a job holding you back and looking for something better. Some were as insignificant as deciding to chew your food at two chomps per second versus four. Regardless of how big or small, all of them put together brought you here, at this moment. If you have dreams of something bigger and that collection of past decisions was not optimal, it has kept you from your dreams to whatever degree. If you are perfectly happy and have reached the potential you seek, then you have done well, and this book was not for you. However, if there is any inkling, large or small, that you could be at a higher level, spiritually, financially, or as a leader, then please read on.

This next step I am going to ask of you can be very intense, and it will take some time to complete, but it is the most impactful thing you will ever do.

We are going to re-write your history to give your future a clear path. You will have some resistance. We have this odd connection to our memories. Changing them on purpose is akin to cutting off your little toe. We feel that all those pictures we have bouncing around in our heads are who we are and that changing them is sacrilegious or taboo at best. Please bear with me, you'll see.

Write out a timeline.

Write down every year that you have been alive with space in between and start filling in the significant events for each year as you remember them. Write down every school you attended in the appropriate year. Write down every home you have lived in, every car you've owned, friends you had at the time, groups you belonged to, jobs you've had, your pet's names, vacations, traumatic events, loss of loved ones, embarrassing moments.

You're making a timeline and laying out your memories on it. You are stringing out your memories on paper, so they are in chronological order. It may be helpful to do this on a computer so you can move the text around as needed. Memories will pop up as you're doing this. Make brief notes next to the date so you can come back to it later.

Example of what this will look like:

1990—Graduated college

1991—Moved to California. Rented house on Main Street with Bill and Tom

1992—Started dating Jenny; first date at the beach

1993—First corporate job at Big Company, Inc
      Car accident the next day. June 3rd.

It will be an ongoing process. If you're 40 years old when you start this, that's 14,600 days' worth of events. There will not be significant things happening every day. The point of this part of the exercise is to jog your memory. Your goal here is to find the days when you made decisions that would affect your life now if you changed them. It could also be a random, non-event day that you pick, but it's more effective to get the impactful days first.

Let's say you do pick a random day. You choose June 20th of 2010 to review. You have no idea what happened that day, but just decide to scan over what might have happened. In your review of how it could have been better, you can determine that was the day you were sitting on the couch, daydreaming about nothing in particular, and then suddenly had an epiphany that would forever change your life and then create your new life from there. If you want your dream life now, you can go back into your past and plant seeds. Your mind has no idea that you're doing this. It doesn't know anything about time.

You can create whatever you want. Break the rules. Make up a new story where aliens came down and decided you were the most interesting Earthling they could find, and they were going to give you a special gift of insight and empathy. The point is to be creative with this—have fun with it. Make sure you broadcast that event forward to the present day and into the future. What would your life be like right now if aliens picked you ten years ago to give the gift of insight? And what would the next ten years be like for you? It's playtime for your brain, but it also sets the stage for your future. Your subconscious mind has no concept of time. It only knows that you are now excited about this idea of being *insightful,* and it will give you more of that because you have told it that is what you are.

As you're working through your timeline, you can also integrate your theme days. Let's say you've already picked *Sexy* as your theme, and you're now reviewing your timeline looking for significant events you can reimagine. You choose the past event of the first time you experienced love at first sight but were too nervous to say anything. She was looking directly at you, and you got scared and looked down at the ground, only to look up a moment later to see her disappointed face as she walked away. Review that memory as if it would have gone better, then do it again even better. Keep on adding details in your favor and draw out the story into the present time and then into the future. When doing these exercises, please don't make it all about you. Make the new memory so it is a benefit for everyone involved.

You can redo this again with a different characteristic from your theme day list. Maybe you pick *creative* for the same memory. When you see this girl for the first time, you say something very creative to her, and she gets all dreamy-eyed over how awesome you are since she thinks of herself as being creative too, and she's now found her soulmate.

This exercise is excellent for your mind on many levels. It breaks down the past decisions and emotions that have cemented themselves into your psyche, most of which you are unaware. It also makes you more creative and able to see patterns for problem-solving. You become less reactionary and more proactive. You'll be less stressed about everything in your life.

You will have moments of despair and angst when you go over tough memories. Make sure you don't stop this exercise until you come to the present time with a better memory. If it's a painful memory, go over this a few times, but spread this exercise out over a few days. Each time you go over it, make sure you come up to present time and into the future with your new, better memory, and always keep improving the memory each time you review it. As mentioned a few times in the book, it will be easier to keep track of your thought process if you either do this aloud or write it down. It'll keep your thoughts in alignment and make it easier to understand. Your new story won't get lost with a drifting mind.

Do this exercise every day. Work on a particular memory until you feel *enlightened* about it, and then move on to the next one. Then watch your new life start to unfold. You'll begin to become the new person that you've laid out for yourself. You've loosened up all the old decisions, opinions, and useless data and let new fresh data that you've hand-picked be part of your life. Have fun!

THE BIG PICTURE

I would like for you to imagine an enlightened future for everyone, not just yourself. We are all connected on a level much more profound than we see on the surface. You can test this on a very small level by staring at someone that does not see you. If they are relatively alert, they will turn and look right at you. Or maybe this has happened to you. You get the strange feeling that someone is staring at you, and you turn to find that they are indeed looking right at you. We are very connected—all living creatures. It is everyone's responsibility to bring us up to a higher level, or at the very minimum, not bring everyone down.

The only way we have a bright future is to move towards an ideal that we all agree on, subconsciously or otherwise. Our future will be one of two diversions. It will be a random future that is a culmination of our current everyday noise or something of our choosing. What you see today is the culmination of mistakes and their solutions. The new solutions are less harmful but still not perfect, so it creates a new problem. Our latest solution creates an additional problem to be solved by yet another patchwork of so-called solutions, so it goes down into history. Our civilization is built upon it. For example, we are still battling with the poor decisions of slavery, nuclear armament, government bureaucracy, taxes, and marketing. Yes, even marketing. Do you need most of the *stuff* you buy, or did clever marketing convince you?

We overburden our minds with useless information. It consumes our mental capacity, and we make poor decisions, which adversely affect those around us, which overburdens their minds. Then they start making poor decisions. With their overburdened minds, they make poor decisions that make the lives worse for those around them. It is a contagion.

Since time immemorial, we have been doing this, and it works to a degree—the evidence is that we are still here. This method does not have a happy ending. It will culminate in more and more poor decisions based on opinions and made-up data that are not valid. Computers will slow this downward spiral, as they can make calculations that we cannot. They can process enormous amounts of data to reveal better choices for us, but this will only soften the blow of our lousy decision-making.

We are a consumer-based civilization. We consume, not just buying stuff, but we consume content and fill our time and heads with *stuff*.

We all have the same organic tools. We all have the same brain, two arms, two legs, two eyes, etc. Yes, there are exceptions, but they are relatively rare. And yet, we are vastly different. There are considerable discrepancies in our abilities to make sound, logical decisions. We're not very bright as a species, and we are more akin to parasites living off the bounty of the planet because of our poor ability to make decisions.

There's a better way for us to think and be. You are the solution. You can lead the way for all of us.

The Review/Preview process laid out in the previous chapter works for you as an individual, and it also works for us as a species and as a society. We all feel the pang of our past. There is a little bit of residual pain in every cell from every bit of trauma we have suffered. If a lion attacked your great great great grandfather, that fear and pain are in you on a cellular level. If your neighbor is a holocaust survivor and creates a bond with you, you connect with her memories on a cellular level. Remember that **EVERY** cell in the Universe came from one original cell—and cells remember the past and each other. Science students routinely test this in class. Take a living cell and damage it with a needle. If you move the needle close to the cell afterward, it will pull away from the threat. It remembers the previous *pain*.

All of us have a responsibility to heal our collective past and our personal history, and we can do this by using the methods laid out in this book. Just as we can follow a course of events into the future to see how it might play out, we can do the reverse and look at where we are today and what circumstances brought us here. The Butterfly Effect works both ways and on all dynamics.

There are multiple dynamics involved. It starts with you as an individual then radiates outward in larger and larger spheres. You are the most important, then those close to you: family and friends. Beyond that would be the small groups you belong to: your company, clubs, and neighbors. Then on a large scale, your country, humanity, all living creatures, the planet, and so on. It is an expansion of Maslow's Hierarchy Scale of Needs, which is only concerned with self-preservation. The need for food, shelter, safety, friends and love, and achieving of one's goals. Considering both scales, the more secure you are with yourself, the more you can take responsibility for the rest of humankind and beyond. If your house is on fire, you are not very likely to help your neighbor with her groceries. If you are embroiled in your life problems, you will not likely put much thought into solving world hunger.

Everything we have created in our civilization is a solution to a problem that would not have existed if we did not consider it a problem in the first place. Remember the Stoics. Problems are a consideration. You becoming wet from the rain is only a problem if you consider it to be one. Complaining you are getting wet does not stop the rain, and it causes problems for those around you who have to listen to it. You could just as easily enjoy the rain.

We only have dentists today to solve a problem caused by a solution to a prior problem. We are the only animal species that has crooked teeth and cavities. Our teeth are crooked because we eat mushy food that is easy to chew and digest. The jaw muscles are the strongest in the body, but they don't get pushed to anything near their capacity. We get cavities because mushy food like bread and sugars get trapped in the little crevices caused by our crooked teeth. We have easy-to-chew food because we became farmers. We became farmers because relatively few people could grow enough food for the entire group, which meant other people had more time to solve different problems. Did you know that before farming, there were no poor people? As humans, we became much more efficient at living, and consequently, some people were left with nothing to do. Some were left behind; some became blacksmiths, carpenters, store owners, and *leaders* (even when we did not need any). Leaders needed something to do to make themselves more important, and the idea of taxes was born. Taxes were initially collected to bolster the egos of those *in charge* and pay for things *they* wanted: palaces, land, and power.

As a civilization, we make mistakes just like we do as individuals. Technically, they are the mistakes of individuals, but the errors are much more impactful to society. If you take responsibility for them as if they were your mistakes, it will give you the power to make that caliber of decision in the future and for humankind's good.

History is fraught with chains of events that lead from one bad decision to the next, and we are still battling with the results. Austria's future king was assassinated while visiting Bosnia. His motorcade took a wrong turn, right into the hands of a member of the Black Hand militia group, who was already plotting to murder him. Two earlier attempts that same day failed, but here he is in an open-air car, rolling directly toward a member of the Black Hand, and purely because the future King's driver took a wrong turn. That one moment started a chain that lead to the rise of Hitler. There are many other factors at play in world events, but my point is that any decision you, a world leader or a terrorist group, make has repercussions that can ripple throughout history. Like how the flapping of a butterfly's wings in Mexico can cause a hurricane in Florida. Sometimes those small innocuous decisions and actions drive the world to change forever. If you are cognizant of those little decisions, you can alter the course of a civilization and a planet.

This cycle has been going on since we started *thinking*. We create a problem, then an imperfect solution, and build on that throughout time. Where does it end?

- June 28th, 1914: Heir to Austria-Hungary's throne assassinated

- Germany and other countries are infuriated

- July 28th, 1914: WWI starts

- 1918: Germany and other countries lose the war

- June 1919-1923: Germany forced to pay reparations—Treaty of Versailles

- 1924: The US grants Germany a loan to help rebuild

- Roaring 20's: US economy booms in post-war enthusiasm

- People have extra money to spend and start investing in the stock market

- Stock-market booms and starts to become over-inflated

- August 1929: Bubble burst—people lose their entire savings and their jobs

- October 1929: Great Depression starts

- The US stops sending money to Germany

- Germany already reeling from the loss of the war and reparations; calling the loan due was the final straw

- German people look desperately for strong leadership

- Enter Hitler

- Holocaust and WWII

You can relieve society's angst on a cellular level, not just for yourself but for all of us. We are all connected on a much deeper level than most realize. Do the Review/Review/Preview method for our collective past. Imagine yourself as Ferdinand's assassin on that hot fateful day in the summer of 1914. You are standing there; the car with the future King of Austria is speeding towards you. They're not supposed to be there. You know your fellow conspirators have failed, and the *mark* has fallen into your lap. How would you have changed that event if you knew that killing him would lead to two world wars and the Holocaust?

You can recreate that event and the entire chain of events that followed. It will relieve the pain and angst that it created, and to some small degree, make us all a little freer. We are all connected. As noted earlier, if you doubt this, stare at someone without them seeing you. Most people will feel it and turn to you to find out what you want. Our connections are profound. Although this will not happen with everyone you try it on. Perhaps some are so thoroughly stuck in their own thoughts, they will never see beyond their nose and will not sense your presence unless you tap them on the shoulder, or maybe they are concentrating on something else at that moment.

Changing the world may seem farfetched, but we are only trying to tip the scales. Life is pretty close to being in balance. We have two major forces, and when they are in harmony, life carries on as intended. We have LIFE and ENTROPY. Life is that thing that animates a cell. It's the difference between a rock and a turtle. It is living and the desire to keep living. Entropy is decay. It's the force that draws the moon closer to the Earth and the Earth to the Sun. It erodes mountains, turns leaves brown, and ages the body. It is death.

The more evolved we become, the more we move away from just taking care of ourselves and into other spheres. If we don't do it considering the life forms just beyond where we are, then our solutions create problems for them. Case in point, we have created a mass extinction. We are killing off more animal species with our poorly thought-out solutions than any other event—ever.

There are three levels to consider as you set out to change how we operate as a civilization.

Pain, Normal, and Pleasure.

- Normal is when entropy and life force are in balance.

- Pain is when entropy is winning.

- Pleasure is when life-force is winning.

Lift is created when you get more pleasure than pain. As in the earlier example about exercising on a smooth gradient, we need to get a little better every day. Keep our society in a balance where we all win, not just you and me, but all living creatures. We can only do this on a cellular level by cleaning up our past. Help me help you.

SUMMARY

I have given you a tremendous number of things to consider and do and be. Here is a quick summary of things to focus on.

- Before bed, pick the theme for the next day from your list of characteristics and mull it over before you go to sleep.

- If you have a big problem you're working to solve or have a creative project, like writing a book, mull it over gently before you go to sleep, and be prepared to write down the first thing that comes to mind in the morning.

- When you wake up, feel the *Theme of the Day*. Before your feet hit the floor when getting out of bed, you should *be* the theme for the day.

- Start your habit stack for the morning.

- Clear the path of your future by previewing what you want to happen, do it, review as if you nailed it, and then preview that into your future. Create a chain of 20-minute segments.

Preview what will happen, do the action, review as if you nailed it, preview yourself continuing into the future, then pick the next 20 minutes and repeat.

- If you start creating stories in your head about something that is bothering you, realize that you noticed and reward yourself, and then start meditating on your theme again. Decide where you need to get more data to solve the problem that is bothering you and stop thinking about it until you get more data.

- Eat if you're getting hungry, especially if you have to make crucial decisions or are about to diverge from your plan.

- Write a rough draft for your day every morning.

- Exercise every day on a gradient until you have the body you want, and then keep doing that routine every day.

- Read lots of books. It not only cuts out Random and Bad input, but it also gives you useful info.

- Cut out bad and random noise and distractions.

- Inflow good stuff and stop the bad inflow.

- Create a clear path to your goals. Go big and think less.

- Push space when you are feeling depressed or introverted.

- Differentiate the paths of a decision you are about to make. How will your future look if you watch tv every evening versus reading a self-help book every evening?

- Pick a pivotal point in history and Review/Review/Preview until you feel good about the event.

Use the fundamental lessons I have taught you here to find a stable base you can launch from. Once you have a base, start to build. Practice the methods I have shown you here. Some, once mastered, you can let go of. Others need to become part of who you are. The mind is the single most powerful thing in the Universe. Take that to heart. Earlier in this book, I mentioned an analogy often used in self-help books about sledding down a hill. The more you go down the hill and use the same grooves as the last time, the harder it is to alter your path. I am asking you first to master making a new path, a different way of thinking. Then I am asking you not to go down the hill at all. Stand on top of that hill and recreate the world.

I happen to know that you did it. I can see you. Every time you look in the mirror, I see you making it happen day by day. You are getting closer. You will make it.

Suppose this book is not for you. Suppose you are completely content with your path and state of affairs. Please pass this along to someone. Help me find its owner.

I promise you, with all my heart and all that I am, that it will light a fire in someone. It will start with a spark, and it will get bigger. And the glow will grow, and that person will create change. They will create an ever-lasting change, and you will benefit. We will all benefit.

I have dedicated my life to making the world a better place. The best way to do that is by helping you gain control of your life, and the best way to do that is to help you master your mind. I have left some tools for you to take advantage of.

Please send me an email and tell me about yourself: stevebode8@ hotmail.com

Thank you,

Steve Bode

The surest and fastest way to see Greatness is to encourage it in others. Please pass the book on to someone you feel could use a boost and see great potential in but are a little lost. You can find more info at www.TheNudge.Club

I would love to hear from you. Please email me with any suggestions, comments, or just to tell me about yourself. stevebode8@ hotmail.com

THANK YOU!

Reviews are very important to me.

I genuinely want to help you, and all that I ask in return is for you to review this book.

If there is anything you don't agree with or would like clarification on, please send me an email. I'd love to hear from you. stevebode8@ hotmail.com

ACKNOWLEDGMENT

Special thanks to some very special people.

Mike Acker for helping grow my business and see my true potential.

Janna Rasch for helping me get all of my grand ideas out of my head and into something comprehensible.

Annabelle Bode for exemplifying everything wonderful about life. Kind, thoughtful, smart, and talented. She's the light of my life— my daughter.

And to Self-Publishing School for making this a reality.